A DECADE IN BORNEO

The Literature of Travel, Exploration and Empire

Series Editors: Iain McCalman and Nicholas Thomas

There is now an unprecedented level of interest in travel, cross-cultural relations and colonial histories. Scholars in cultural history, literary studies, art history, anthropology and related fields have become increasingly interested in the history of encounters between Europeans and other peoples, in the intellectual and scientific dimensions of exploration and travel, and in the development of travel-writing genres.

Despite this burgeoning scholarly interest, many important texts are unavailable, or available only in expensive facsimiles that lack up-to-date commentary. This new series makes key texts more widely available, including not only remarkable but previously unpublished or poorly known texts, but also new editions of well-known works. Accessible introductions situate the works in the light of recent historical and anthropological research, and theoretical developments in the understanding of travel and colonial representation; annotations provide relevant contextual information and emphasize questions of interpretation.

Published titles:

Maiden Voyages and Infant Colonies: Two Women's Travel Narratives of the 1790s, edited by Deirdre Coleman

George Barrington, *George Barrington's Voyage to Botany Bay* (*c.* 1793), edited by Suzanne Rickard

George Keate, *An Account of the Pelew Islands* (1788), edited by Nicholas Thomas and Karen L. Nero

Forthcoming titles include:

F. E. Maning, *Old New Zealand and Other Writings* (1863), edited by Alex Calder

Hester Lynch Piozzi, *Observations and Reflections Made in the Course of a Journey Through France, Germany and Italy* (1789), edited by Chloe Chard

David Samwell, *The Death of Captain Cook and Other Writings* (1786), edited by Iain McCalman, Martin Fitzpatrick and Nicholas Thomas

C. F. Volney, *Ruins, or a Survey of the Revolutions of Empire* (*c.* 1791), edited by Iain McCalman

For further information, see
www.anu.edu.au/culture/projects/cultural_history.html

A Decade in Borneo

Ada Pryer

Edited by Susan Morgan

Leicester University Press
London and New York

Leicester University Press
A Continuum imprint
The Tower Building, 11 York Road, London, SE1 7NX
370 Lexington Avenue, New York, NY 10017–6503

First published 2001

British Library Cataloguing-in-Publication Data
A catalogue record for this book is available from the British Library.

ISBN 0-7185-0197-7 (hardback)

Library of Congress Cataloguing-in-Publication Data
Pryer, Ada.
 A decade in Borneo / Ada Pryer; edited by Susan Morgan.
  p. cm. – (Literature of travel, exploration, and empire)
 Previously published: 1894.
 Includes bibliographical references and index.
 ISBN 0-7185-0197-7
  1. Borneo—Description and travel. 2. Pryer, Ada—Journeys—Borneo.
 I. Morgan, Susan, 1943— II. Title. III. Series.

DS646.312.P79 2001
959.5′303–dc21   00-055656

Editorial work towards this publication has been supported by

the centre for cross-cultural research
AN AUSTRALIAN RESEARCH COUNCIL SPECIAL RESEARCH CENTRE
THE AUSTRALIAN NATIONAL UNIVERSITY, CANBERRA, ACT 0200
www.anu.edu.au/culture

Typeset by BookEns Ltd, Royston, Herts
Printed and bound in Great Britain by Biddles Ltd, Guildford and King's Lynn

CONTENTS

ILLUSTRATIONS

Plate 1
Cover of original edition of *A Decade in Borneo*, Kelly & Walsh Ltd, Hongkong, Shanghai, Yokohama and Singapore, 1893.

Plate 2
Edward Weller, 'Borneo', *Weekly Dispatch Atlas*, 1880. *Source:* National Library of Australia, Canberra.

Plate 3
G. McCulloch, 'The Sea Dyaks', lithograph, from Spenser St John, *Life in the Forests of the Far East: Travels in Sabah and Sarawak in the 1860s*, London, 1873. *Source:* National Library of Australia, Canberra.

Plate 4
T. Ficken, 'The City of Brunei – Sunset', lithograph, from Spenser St John, *Life in the Forests of the Far East: Travels in Sabah and Sarawak in the 1860s*, London, 1873. *Source:* National Library of Australia, Canberra.

Plate 5
'Elopura (Sandakan)', unattributed engraving, 1883. *Source:* Sabah Museum, Sabah, Malaysia.

Plate 6
'District Officer's House, Mempakul', photographer unknown. *Source:* Sabah Museum, Sabah, Malaysia.

Plate 7
T. Ficken, 'View from Near the Rahjah's Cottage', lithograph, from Spenser St John, *Life in the Forests of the Far East: Travels in Sabah and Sarawak in the 1860s*, London, 1873. *Source:* National Library of Australia, Canberra.

ACKNOWLEDGEMENTS

It has required the support and attention of many thoughtful people to bring this little book to readers once again. I first thank Miami University of Ohio for the financial support so necessary to completing such a project. I am particularly grateful to Ross Shanley-Roberts for his cheerful ingenuity in rescuing me from technological limbo by scanning the original text not once but twice, and to Carol Willeke for providing not only the funding but the explanation of the mechanics of the funding which allowed me to complete the edition at last. At Australian National University, Nicholas Thomas welcomed me, and Ada Pryer, to the series with an informed interest and enthusiasm, and Christine Winter has been consistently helpful in following through with practical information. Great support also came from the Australian National University, and from Jenny Newell, who answered my months of queries with grace as well as precision, who tracked down illustrations for me, and who made a discussion of how Australians use commas seem friendly and fun. Finally, I thank Janet Joyce, my editor at Continuum, for those best of all qualities in an editor – tactful intelligence and great patience.

Introduction

From the 1870s on, the British slowly took over the states on the Malay Peninsula, effectively inventing Malaya. The takeover process was characterized, among other qualities, by a localized imperial rhetoric which was as conflicted as it was inventive. The British increased their territorial control with a declared reluctance which was continually overcome by an even more forcefully declared desire to provide what was called the stability and order necessary for profitable enterprise. To many business-minded imperial voices, perhaps the most famous being those of Frank Swettenham and Isabella Bird, local politics and customs, for all their charms, could in the end be explained as economic indicators of disorder. What was good for business turned out to be what was understood and described as the familiar predictability of British control.

British Malaya did increasingly provide riches for England, from tin and then from rubber, producing, in a famous phrase, 'wealth beyond the dreams of avarice'.[1] The adjacent island of Borneo did not. But this was not for lack of trying. Like British Malaya, Borneo was the object of a pattern of contradictory public positions that would serve to determine its imperial history. The gaps between much of British rhetoric and British actions in Borneo turned out to be even wider than in British Malaya. Yet there were some unique aspects to the battles between British words and British presences in Borneo. Perhaps the most important was the existence of a vocal and powerful group who were against the notion of economic development of the island at all. For several decades, what blocked development of the northern part of the island (the south having been occupied by the Dutch) was not only the familiar, general policy of anti-expansionism but also a frequently announced Colonial Office opinion that a sustained British presence in Borneo would be a major financial mistake. It would not make money; it would require money. Yet, despite these recurrent, insistent and economically persuasive arguments on the side of a non-interventionist policy, the British government approved a government-monitored commercial Charter for North Borneo in

December 1881. And in 1888 the government officially took over not only North Borneo but also the adjacent sites of Brunei and Sarawak as British protectorates.

The Charter was particularly surprising because it was a Liberal government that approved it, having been returned to power in the spring of 1880. The Liberals were led by William Gladstone, the renowned anti-imperialist, who had referred to chartered companies 'with their "death-like shadow" as being "the greatest obstacles to the well-being of colonies"', and long argued that expansion had 'weakened the Empire'.[2] Gladstone would later claim publicly that he could not remember ever having seen, much less approved, the Borneo Papers, and wondered if they had really been submitted to the Cabinet and discussed there at all. But he was not much upset, and as Prime Minister even defended the Charter against Tory complaints in Parliament.[3] Gladstone's position was that this particular commercial charter would cause no trouble or expense for the government. The 1888 takeovers were to prove him wrong. How did this reluctant expansionism in Borneo come about? That story is also the story of how and why William and Ada Pryer were in Borneo.

WHY BORNEO?

The British interest in Borneo had everything to do with its location, which in the nineteenth century meant where it was situated relative to other places of imperial interest. Borneo's initial geographic and economic value for the British was not that of a location in itself at all, but as somewhere *en route* to somewhere else. Generally, up to the mid-nineteenth century the single overriding significance to the British of all the lands which we now know as Southeast Asia was not their lands but their waters, the shipping routes between India and China. The states between India and China were simply that, states between, crucial because a huge number of commercial vessels passed through their waters trading goods between China and India (and from India on to England and the rest of Europe).

Protecting the enormously lucrative China trade – from the French in the waters south of their colonies in Cochin-China, from the Dutch coming north from the Indies islands, including southern Borneo, and from the various Malay 'pirates' and other regional peoples in that crucial waterway between the Malay Peninsula and Borneo – drove British policy in the region. Borneo, as the largest island in what was called the East Indies, that immense series of islands stretching from the southern tip of the Malay Peninsula on into the Pacific towards China and Australia, mattered to the British quite simply because its long north and west coasts bordered on the South China Sea.[4] The coastal waters of this third largest of the world's islands were full of inlets and tiny islands where raiders, European as well as regional, could hide.

There were other reasons besides sea pirates for the increasing British interest during the mid-nineteenth century in the strategic value of North Borneo in supporting the China trade. The British navy had adopted steam by the 1820s, though it did not completely abandon sail until 1870. The changeover from sail to steam was driven largely by increasing competition with other nations for the China trade, a competition which required faster and faster ships. But if steam guaranteed greater and more reliable speed it also required lots of coal, and that meant coaling stations along the sea routes. In addition, since the trade with China increased enormously by the 1850s after the so-called 'opium wars' by which the British forced China into acceding to the drug trade, so did the sheer numbers of ships in the South China Sea. Already by 1842, in order to protect commercial convoys, the Admiralty had virtually permanently 'allotted fifteen ships to the East Indies and China Station'.[5] By the second half of the nineteenth century the South China Sea was becoming quite a busy place.

The many ships filling the South China Sea at this time were not just those of the British or local peoples. The Americans were there, also trading to China in their fast clippers which could beat the British Indiamen until the British learned to build even faster teak clippers themselves. The French were there, building up their colonial empire on the mainland just east of Siam and to the north of the South China Sea, in what they called Cochin-China. The Dutch, of course, controlled a great deal of the region, particularly south of Singapore (at the southern tip of the Malay Peninsula) in the islands composing what was called the Malay or Eastern Archipelago or, more familiarly, the East Indies. The Anglo–Dutch Treaty of 1824 had been a convenient agreement to divide up the regions of Southeast Asia between two acquisitive parties which didn't actually have rights to any of the region. Eschewing the risks and costs of competition, the two simply drew an imaginary geographical line and each took half. The British got Singapore and whatever was north of it, and Holland was able to claim everything south of Singapore. Of the three largest islands of the Indies, the Dutch had their major port at Batavia, now Jakarta, on the island of Java, controlled much of Sumatra, and had taken the huge southern portion of Borneo (now Kalimantan). The Spanish were very much present as well. Having taken the islands of the

Philippines, they were busy during the 1870s and early 1880s in a lengthy effort also to take the Sulu Archipelago, the small islands located between the Philippines and Borneo. Even the Germans and the Austrians sent a few ships, though the German interest in acquiring imperial territories in Southeast Asia was to develop a little later.

In this commercial relay race back and forth between China, India and Europe, it occurred to almost everybody that controlling the land would be a way of controlling the sea. One result was that Borneo's strategic location along the shipping route to China created a complex history and geography. In the first decade of the twenty-first century the island is split up among three countries: Malaysia in the north (the two states of Sarawak on the northwest coast and Sabah at the top – the two together bigger than the rest of Malaysia), Brunei a dot between Sarawak and Sabah, and Indonesia, comprising all the rest of the island (the state of Kalimantan). In the nineteenth century, as a result of both European and regional aggression, Borneo was even more divided. At various times, it was part Dutch (Kalimantan), part Malayo-Muslim (Brunei), part non-Malay tribes (when and where the foreigners weren't land grabbing), part British Protectorate (Sarawak, then also Brunei and North Borneo), part British colony (the small island of Labuan, just off the west coast), part British commercial property (British North Borneo), and part privately owned by an Englishman (Sarawak).

In establishing a position about Borneo, British public rhetoric was driven by explicit doubts as to its economic feasibility combined with a sense that its major value was the location of its coastline. More generally, the goal of the British imperial enterprise 'repeatedly laid out by policy makers in London was not the acquisition of large amounts of territory – an idea repugnant to successive colonial secretaries, but the possession of strategically located small naval stations and entrepots'.[6] In keeping with this governmental position, in an 1847 treaty with the Sultan of Brunei, the British acquired the tiny island of Labuan, just off the northwest coast of Borneo. Their first effort to establish a trading station off Borneo had been the island of Balambangan in 1773, which they only really held for two years, and officially abandoned in 1805. Possessing Labuan at last fulfilled British Colonial Office perceptions of everything the British needed from the area around Borneo. The minuscule island didn't have any territory to speak of, but did provide a strategically located port in the China Seas from which the Royal Navy could patrol those all-important waterways to China. But in spite of government statements and policies and opinions, there would be no stopping with Labuan. Acquiring this little island turned out to be the beginning rather than the end of official British takeovers in the region.

Many of the British government's problems in the region were to come from the fact that, unofficially, the British had been established in Borneo well before 1847. The whole notion of the lack of a British territorial presence had been a fiction, though a particularly favoured fiction, since the early 1840s. Indeed, much of the support for the British acquisition of Labuan had come from an Englishman already living in Borneo, who arranged the takeover and was appointed the first Governor of Labuan: Sir James Brooke. Brooke lived and ruled in Sarawak, a state stretching along the all-important northwest coast of Borneo. His position, and his extensive influence, helped in key ways to shape North Borneo.

Sarawak was one of the southern states in the Sultanate of Brunei, rather distant from the influence of the Sultan and his court. In 1842 the Sultan appointed Brooke to be the Governor, or Raja, of the Brunei state of Sarawak. Inspired by the story of Raffles and Singapore, Brooke had been looking for a private venture in order to establish a British presence around Borneo. His appointment fulfilled a pledge made by the Sultan's second in command: to give Brooke the governorship of this small state if he could successfully end a rebellion there. Brooke agreed to pay the Sultan an annual fee out of the tax revenue he could collect.

Then in 1843 the Sultan, almost certainly intimidated by the presence of a flotilla of visiting British ships (Brooke having good friends in the Royal Navy), granted this British Raja the right to name his own heirs. James Brooke thus gained control of Sarawak in perpetuity. In fact there would be only three 'White Rajahs', and only two of them were active rulers. Charles Brooke, younger son of James' sister, became Rajah at James' death in 1868. James himself never married, though he appears to have had sexual relationships with Malay and tribal women, and also acknowledged one British illegitimate son.[7]

In the early 1860s James disinherited the declared heir to Sarawak, the older son of his sister, who had already been acting Rajah, in favour of her second son, Charles. The second 'White Rajah' pursued the dreams and policies of the first with, if possible, even more enthusiasm than his uncle. In 1917 Charles died, and his oldest son, Vyner Brooke, became the third and last Rajah. Vyner broke family tradition in that he did not rule the same way as his two famous ancestors. The Japanese held Sarawak during the Second World War, and in 1946 Vyner gave it to England as a Crown Colony. Along with North Borneo, Sarawak became Britain's last colonial acquisition. The history of the two states had been intertwined for a century, in a continuing struggle for dominance, both territorial and symbolic, of the British territories in Borneo.

The problem of Sarawak

Sarawak is a rare, and perhaps unique, phenomenon in the nineteenth-century history of British imperial interventions. It was a British colony in a continually contested sense, but not by any legal or public designation. It was a country as private property. But what, after all, is that? Throughout the second half of the nineteenth century Sarawak was a continual problem for England. The basic issue, in spite of all its complexities, was precisely the political location, the anomalous international legal status of Sarawak. Was it a nation, or a state within a nation? And if it was a nation, was it colonized by England or not? The White Rajahs wanted Britain to recognize it officially as an independent country, which would have pitted the weight of British naval power against Brunei.[8] The British government repeatedly refused to do so, in part because Sarawak's anomalous status allowed the Colonial Office the fiction of not being involved in the acquisition of territory in Borneo, and in part because it was unacceptable to the sovereignty of England that a British subject should also be head of a foreign state. Moreover, one of the government's frequently declared reasons accompanying its rejections of the Brookes' frequent importunings was British official awareness that to recognize the sovereignty of Sarawak was to violate the sovereignty of Brunei to which the state technically belonged, however much the Brookes preferred, and argued, otherwise.

As early as 1846 in his letter to the Admiralty, Lord Palmerston of the Foreign Office was quite explicit in his reasons for trying to limit the extent to which the Royal Navy could help James Brooke sustain and extend his rule in Borneo by fighting the coastal raiders. Brooke's cunning but dubious argument in asking for help was that the Navy had to protect him and the other British in Sarawak as British subjects. After all, the government did acknowledge that 'the Existence of Sarawak, ruled as it was by a British subject, did serve Britain's interests in so far that it excluded other Powers from the area'.[9] None the less, Palmerston reminded the Admiral that 'Your Lordships are aware that it has not been the wish of Her Majesty's Government that British Subjects should possess territory on the mainland of Borneo'.[10] The government was still arguing the same point in 1858, refusing to make Sarawak a Protectorate on the sensible grounds that

> if every English subject were to be allowed to settle in any district he might think fit, and then afterwards to call upon the Government as a matter of right to give him military and civil protection ... it must lead the Government into endless difficulties and expenditure.[11]

In terms of the question of British acquisition of territory, a continuing problem which the Brookes and Sarawak posed for British foreign policy was their active commitment to expansion. From the 1850s on, the first two Sarawak White Rajahs pursued what Wright has aptly dubbed an 'absorption policy', annexing more and more of the river states of Brunei.[12] They did it in a variety of ways: by tricks of diplomacy, by magnifying minor incidents as threatening to either British lives or native rights or both, or simply by moving into a state and declaring it theirs. A measure of their success is that Sarawak increased from less than 5,000 square kilometres in 1841 to its present size of 125,000 square kilometres.[13] Obviously, one way to push back the political barriers to the sovereignty of Sarawak was to do so literally, by taking over, and becoming the sovereign of, Brunei. If Brunei ruled Sarawak, as the British government was given to insisting, then the Brookes could get the government to recognize their claims to Sarawak by themselves ruling Brunei. The Brookes came very close to this stated goal, though in the end, because the British government intervened, they did not succeed.

Yet the limits to Britain's willingness to honour Brunei sovereignty above the claims of one of their own were strikingly marked in 1860. When James Brooke's two nephews, Charles and his brother, quite illegally invaded the Brunei province of Mukah, the British Governor of Labuan, arguing that they 'as British subjects came under his consular jurisdiction', ordered them to lay down their arms and leave Brunei territory.[14] The response from the British government when appealed to by an outraged James Brooke was telling. The Foreign Office officially rebuked the Governor of Labuan, and the Colonial Office not only removed him from his post but officially called him home in disgrace. 'It was one thing to leave Rajah Brooke in a legal never-never land without official British support, but it was quite another matter to turn the full weight of British authority against an English gentleman.'[15] The Brooke nephews were delighted, and immediately travelled to Brunei, where they demanded and got the territory of Mukah. The now helpless Sultan was forced to recognize that the British, when it came to one of their own, were not going to give him the protection from territorial aggressors that he had been promised by the treaty of 1847.

Finally, Britain did move to declare the remaining territory of Brunei, as well as Sarawak, a British Protectorate in 1888. They did so in good part because it seemed to be the only way the Sultan and the British government had left to keep Brunei in existence without the unacceptable option of the British actually fighting against 'an English gentleman'. Due to Sarawak's aggressions, by 1888 there was almost nothing left of Brunei – except, of course, some oil, discovered in 1903.

In pursuit of the cause of recognition outside Sarawak, of being given their 'real' name, James Brooke might well be accused of relentless ambition, and the methods of Charles Brooke have been described by a recent historian as 'ruthless double-dealing and blackmail'.[16] Not surprisingly, such evaluations do not characterize the image of the White Rajahs sustained by most of the historians recording the Brookes' rule in Sarawak. The White Rajahs, and the country they claimed they owned, attained what I would call a mythic significance in Victorian imperial discourse. Its lack of economic identity may have been the most striking point about this would-be nation. In opposition to British proceedings in the Malay Peninsula, the Brookes discouraged British commercial activities in Sarawak and actively blocked European investments which would take their profits at the expense of native interests. It wasn't at all clear that Sarawak even had many natural resources to 'develop'. The Brookes were not motivated by material greed. Rajah Charles railed at 'these times when eager speculators are always seeking for some new place to exploit ... when the white man comes to the fore and the dark coloured is thrust to the wall and when capital rules and justice ceases'.[17] The 'meaning' of Sarawak had to be located on a different ideological ground from the all too common one of some kind of intertwining of European superiority with the right to systems of economic exploitation. Nor was it territory, any more than commercial profits, which drove the Brookes. In spite of their almost ceaseless efforts to control more land, they actively discouraged any kind of British settlement, and continually insisted that the state must exist to serve its own indigenous tribes.

In 1854, Harriette McDougall, wife of the first Bishop of Sarawak, published *Letters From Sarawak; Addressed to a Child*, a book she had sent in sections to her son at school in England. Sarawak, she says, 'has for the last seven years furnished a romance to the English public, which for a time made its Rajah a favourite hero'.[18] How long that 'romance' would last may be suggested by another account over a century later, by a would-be historian of Sarawak in 1960.

> In all history only one man succeeded in coming from the West and making himself king over an Eastern race, and founding a dynasty which lasted for a hundred years. ... He lived a life such as schoolboys dream of. ... He looked like a romantic hero, and behaved like one.[19]

The romance that Sarawak 'furnished' to fulfil the dreams of English schoolboys lay precisely in justifying the taking of territory as a matter of individual heroism, this 'archetypal fantasy of isolated white men ruling over savages in a tropical setting'.[20] What Sarawak and the ongoing debate about its identity offered to British imperial and racist interests was the possibility that an individual Englishman could go anywhere and become anything, could conquer pirates by sea and defeat jungle tribes by land, could find for himself his very own country and become its king. He could do this not only in an eighteenth-century novel like *Robinson Crusoe* but in real life. An Englishman could have 'a little kingdom carved out for himself'.[21] In the words of Joseph Conrad's Marlow, narrator in the novel which was almost certainly inspired by the history of the White Rajahs, the romance come true of Sarawak represented the heroic fantasies of Lord Jim, who 'had beheld the face of that opportunity which, like an Eastern bride, had come veiled to his side'.[22]

This particular legend was 'at its best in boys' adventure stories of the early twentieth century when the European imperial system was at its zenith'.[23] Brooke's Sarawak, that veiled 'eastern bride' of European dreams, was not only Lord Jim's Patusan, in a novel dazzling in its insights into and critique of the genre of imperial adventure story, but also Kim's India and Peter Pan's Never Never Land. The White Rajahs were a fantasy come to life, a dream come true. Never Never Land could be found on a chart, on the west coast of Borneo; and so, quite literally, could Conrad's Patusan, an actual village in a part of Brunei which the White Rajahs took over. The Brookes' story became the story of all 'our' possibilities, of the individualist promise at the heart of the imperial enterprise. Once the boy was cast as a man who lit out for the territory, all that remained was to present the specifics of what that dream consisted of and what its fulfilment was actually like. The narratives had to fill in the details, and send back the information from that fabulous reality. It is surely no coincidence that the first book by the writer who described Sarawak as 'furnish[ing] a romance' to the British public was cast in the form of letters to an English schoolboy.

A ROYAL CHARTER FOR NORTH BORNEO

By the mid-1870s the Foreign Office was seeing the two British presences in Borneo – in Labuan and in Sarawak – as real problems. Charles Brooke had many supportive friends for his ambitions in the Colonial Office, while those in the Foreign Office tended to view him as both aggressive and untrustworthy and to view his plans to rule North Borneo as not in England's commercial interests. Labuan was simply recognized by all as a failure. It had not developed into an active port, had not even become self-sufficient, and had failed to make a profit on its own coal-mines at a time when coal was much in demand. By 1888 there were to be fewer than ten Europeans still living on the island.[24] In the 1870s, with support gone for developing Labuan, a general sense that Brooke really needed to be reined in, and, with the ever-increasing naval presences around Borneo of other European powers, several members of the government began to believe that the answer to these problematic presences was, incredibly, yet a third British presence in North Borneo.

The belief, contradicting so many official and public positions, was driven by some simple political facts. The Americans were already there. In 1865 Charles Moses, the United States Consul in Brunei, had received (with promises of paying for them later) concessions from the Sultan of Brunei for North Borneo for the next ten years. The Sultan was agreeable largely because it was suspected the Americans might do what the British had so far failed to do, despite all their public statements. A significant American presence in North Borneo might halt Brooke's territorial expansions. Moses immediately went to Hong Kong and sold the concessions – though retaining some rights – to two American merchants, Joseph Torrey and Thomas Harris and their two Chinese partners. The four established 'The American Trading Company of Borneo', gathered an eager group, and set off to establish a settlement in North Borneo. By the end of two years however, Harris and others had died and the settlement had failed. In 1875, just before the concessions were about to lapse, Torrey sold them to Baron von Overbeck in Hong Kong. Overbeck, who was born in Germany, had emigrated as a young man to America, worked as a whaler in Honolulu, and then as a successful businessman in Hong Kong. He had been awarded a barony for professional services by the Austrian government and was their Consul in Hong Kong at the time.

Overbeck and Torrey travelled to Brunei, where the Sultan's heir tentatively renewed the concessions for another ten years (the Sultan refused to 'renew' anything, since he had never been paid in the first place). Overbeck then travelled to London to raise capital for this venture and persuaded Alfred Dent to join. Overbeck returned to Brunei with Dent's money and paid the Sultan on 29 December 1877. The Sultan then officially signed the new concession agreement, ceding his northern territories to Overbeck and Dent.

There were a couple of problems. First, only in the most theoretical sense could it be said that the territories were the Sultan's to cede. Brunei was a small and fairly poor state, its glory days 200 years in the past, and its rule of the huge northern lands of Borneo mostly a faded memory. Brunei's resources for ruling its peoples had been virtually used up in efforts to stave off foreign invasions, particularly in the nineteenth century by the ever-encroaching Brookes. Moreover, the east side of the northern territories was claimed by another Sultan, with a more present-day right to that claim. The Sultan of Sulu, the archipelago just east of Borneo, claimed the whole northeastern section of Borneo. His ownership was fairly widely acknowledged, but his rule there was weak, also due to his energies and resources being used up in efforts to beat back foreign aggression. The piracy of this region 'was mainly a symptom of the breakdown of law and order as the sultanates of Brunei and Sulu were reduced to impotence'.[25] The Sultan of Sulu was engaged in a long and costly defensive war to beat back the Spanish from taking his territories now that they had the islands just east of his archipelago, the Philippines. Northeast Borneo was crucial to him, not least because, being the western part of his territories, it could be somewhere to escape to if he lost the rest of his lands to Spain.

Overbeck handled the dual claims of the two sultans quite simply. He went directly from Brunei to Jolo, the main island in the Sulu Archipelago. Having signed the concession with one Sultan, he proceeded to sign the concession with the other, and paid him too. But there was one difference in the terms. While stopping in Labuan, Overbeck had met the British Colonial Secretary there, William Hood Treacher. Treacher was delighted that the proposal for commercial development of North Borneo was being revived, and with British capital by a well-known British business firm. He was not aware that Dent and Overbeck saw this as only an investment, and planned to sell the concessions as soon as the sultans had signed. Treacher went with Overbeck to Sulu, lending the influence of the British government to Overbeck's request. This was important, because the Sultan of Sulu was persuaded to sign the concessions once he saw them as carrying the weight of the British government. He would not be giving up his one escape route from the Spanish to some private trading company but, he hoped, would be putting the protective might of England at his back. His idea, which proved to be correct, was that the Spanish would not overrun the east coast of North Borneo with the British flag flying there.

Treacher did not lend the support of his government position to this private enterprise for nothing; he wanted something for England as well. Treacher lent his 'influence', and in return Overbeck included a clause in the concessions treaty that the ceded territories could not be transferred to another party without the permission of the British government. In other words, Dent and Overbeck could no longer sell their cessions to just anyone who was willing to pay. In spite of British control, Rajah Brooke, predictably, was outraged, having long considered all of North Borneo effectively, if not yet officially, as his. Finding himself in the odd position of suddenly being the moral opponent of territorial takeovers, Brooke wrote to Treacher threatening to do his utmost 'to thwart the encroachments of this wild and unjustifiable adventure'.[26]

The British government, of course, only wanted a British company in Borneo. Again, they could deny that this was British acquisition of territory. It was simply private enterprise, albeit with a few government guidelines to protect Britain from those other encroaching European nations. The next step was inevitable. Dent realized he and Overbeck could not simply turn over the cessions for a quick profit; they would have to develop the place. Dent bought out Overbeck and proceeded to use his and Treacher's extensive connections, particularly Dent's friendship with Sir Julian Pauncefote, Permanent Under-Secretary, to apply for a Royal Charter. During the three years of political manoeuvring that it finally took to be granted a Charter, Dent had secured financial as well as political support for this enterprise, and instead of his single ownership there was what was officially called a 'Provisional Association' composed of investors. In November 1881 the Charter was granted, and the Association changed its name. The British North Borneo Company, also called the BNBC, or also the North Borneo Chartered Company (NBCC), began.

Events in North Borneo had not kept pace with the long and unpredictable process of applying for and receiving a Royal Charter. The plan for a Charter had been something of a long shot by Dent as he faced the financial implications of the clause which Treacher had Overbeck include in his treaty with the Sultan of Sulu. But whether or not it would have the special backing of a government charter there could still be a commercial company, but one that couldn't be sold without government approval. When Overbeck returned to Brunei with Dent's capital and then travelled on to Sulu, he had been prepared for success. His plan was to divide the northern territories into three commercial sections, each with a resident and trading centre: the west, the middle and the east. After successfully concluding his business with the Sultan of Sulu he stopped first to establish the company's station on the east coast of the northern territories, in Sandakan Bay. There he left behind someone who had travelled with him through the signing of the concession treaties, a young man who had worked in the Philippines and had been a bookkeeper for the Shanghai firm of Thorne and Company. He was to be the representative of the BNBC for its eastern section. Overbeck gave him the official title of 'Resident of the East Coast' and, for good measure, Treacher named him British Consular Agent. The young man, William Pryer, landed in Sandakan Bay on 11 February 1878.

THE ENTHUSIAST

When Overbeck left William Pryer in Sandakan Bay that February day, accompanied by two Eurasian assistants, ten Chinese labourers and one West Indian servant, the first thing Pryer did was to fly the flag; two flags, actually: the flag of Dent Brothers, and the Union Jack. Pryer would remain 'Resident of the East Coast' for three years, until Treacher returned with an official appointment of Governor of the eastern section. Pryer's service as British Consular Agent was a little shorter. In spite of Treacher's claim that Pryer's use of the British flag 'should cause no misconception', Treacher was reprimanded for overstepping his authority when he returned to Labuan, and Pryer's government title was rescinded.[27]

William Pryer occupies a permanent place in British imperial mythology about the British takeover of the lands of Southeast Asia. What Pryer offered the British public, the government and private investors was an appealing alternative of colonial enterprise to the aggressive adventurer image cultivated by the Rajah Brookes. Pryer's life would come to stand for colonialism as peaceful rule, for non-aggression, and, best of all, for a commitment to economic development as the ultimate justification for acquiring foreign territories. Whether or not this representation of his life is true, it certainly functioned as 'true' in the public rhetoric which drove the British nation's acceptance of its policies of imperialism.

Born in London on 7 March 1843, William Burgess Pryer began travelling with Overbeck when he was aged 34 and was to land in Sandakan less than a month before his thirty-fifth birthday. His reputation is largely based on the fact that once he settled in northeast Borneo he stayed there for the rest of his life (with two or three trips back to England) and promoted British commercial interests. As Joseph Hatton, invoking all the familiar colonial stereotypes in one of the two obituaries published in the *British North Borneo Herald* put it, Pryer was

> a typical British pioneer, and the British pioneer is not the fire-eater some of our foreign neighbours seem to imagine, nor is he the kind of hero the romantic novelist loves to paint him. On the contrary, he

is gentle, modest, quiet, unassuming. Yet, brave as he is unassuming, and enthusiastic as he is modest.

(16 March 1899, p. 92)

The earlier obituary was a little less heavy-handed, more simple. Certainly, it argued for the greatness of 'one of the earliest pioneers of foreign enterprize in British North Borneo'. It informed us that Pryer was a man 'of splendid physique and remarkable for his personal fearlessness' (1 February, p. 44). Perhaps rather more accurately, on the subject of Pryer's enthusiasm we are informed that

> his chief fault was a little too much enthusiasm, but he had an undoubted faith in the future of the Territory and did his best to aid it, though his comments on policy and procedure were not at all times pleasing to the authorities.

Pryer was an enthusiast who grew up during the major age of British imperialism and developed an interest in that familiar Victorian pair: science and adventure. Something of an amateur naturalist, he had 'explored' and collected butterflies in the Philippines before signing on with Dent and Overbeck and moving to Borneo. Convinced of the great potential of the huge northern territories, Pryer spent the first few years settling the company as an authority over the areas that he could reach and influence. That authority had to do both with conditions in Sabah and the state of affairs of this particular private enterprise.

From the first, the company was hugely undercapitalized and understaffed. This is perhaps the most significant and continuing fact about the British North Borneo Company, and meant that, from the very beginning and continuing for decades, there could be no question of this company actually engaging directly in commerce, in the production, trade or sale of goods. Thus, from the very beginning, the company became of necessity an administrative enterprise, a 'company' only in the sense that it claimed the right through the sultans' concessions to collect tariffs and taxes on goods, by 1901 even licensing all – even the tiniest – boats. These ongoing financial constraints inevitably limited the possibility of profit, and there weren't even enough staff to collect the tariff and tax money. Of necessity, Pryer and the company employed many local people as their 'agents' in the field. The 'company' was, of course, a government rather than a business.

To the peoples who lived there, North Borneo was divided, named and understood in terms of rivers. By the 1870s, when Pryer arrived, the virtually non-existent authority of Brunei, and the off-on authority of Sulu, as the two kingdoms struggled against their own foreign aggressors, had allowed the regions of North Borneo to become havens for warring groups. The local peoples had abandoned many of the settlements at the mouths of the rivers as too vulnerable to visiting ships looking for supplies any way they could get them, and retreated many miles upriver into the interior. Pryer's control of river traffic at the mouths of rivers did result in peoples again building villages where the rivers met the seas, but the interior peoples were probably worse off than they had been before the advent of the company. Villages were at the mercy of those locals who claimed to be – and often actually were – the company's agents, but agents without accountability who could forcibly collect whatever charges they wanted.

William Pryer's enthusiasm for company policies carried him through the first few years, during which those policies were inevitably shaped by the crushing disparities between the scarcity of the money available and the vast lands to be policed. Here is an account of him, published anonymously in *The British North Borneo Herald* in 1883:

> Pryer, a busy and enthusiastic soul, would periodically enliven our midday conferences with his latest 'discovery' in Borneo's assets ... he was a very charming and likeable man. An ex-amateur champion boxer, utterly fearless with man or beast; a magician with snakes, the collection of which he made a hobby, he once seriously upset the nerves of a party of officers of *H. M. S. Magpie* he had taken for a walk in the jungle after lunch. he was leading us, talking, when he suddenly dived into some undergrowth shouting 'grab his tail!' – and while we started, he suddenly reappeared plunging about grasping a 20 foot python by the neck.[28]

Later in the same article Pryer is said to claim to be sending yet another snake to the London Zoo, alive.

For Pryer, 1883 was a wonderful year for several reasons. Mr von Donop, in his public diary of travelling in Sabah in 1882 and 1883, seems to have caught the general excitement of a possible commercial frontier, claiming that 'North Borneo is just now like a beehive'.[29] He points out that town lots in Sandakan are selling at high prices, that people are starting tobacco and sugar plantations, that the first newspaper, the *British North Borneo Herald* is about to start publishing, and that two resthouses have even been opened.

Von Donop ends his diary with an exciting 'P.S. – Ladies are beginning to come to Sandakan, and more I am informed are expected'. One of these was Ada, whom William married on 10 December 1883. He was 40 and she was 28. Ada Blanche Locke had been born on 25 October 1855, in St

Woolos (Newport), Monmouth, in what was then the west of England but is now officially Wales. Her father, Edward Locke, originally from Gloucestershire, was an engineer in a local nail factory, most probably the DOS factory in Newport. Her mother, Mary, who had been born in Middlesex, was much younger (by about seventeen years) than her father, a pattern Ada followed in marrying William. The family was clearly middle-class, though hardly distinguished, and they lived quietly in Maindee, a part of Newport. Edward and Mary were never to leave Maindee, and were buried there.

After the early exhilarating years of being on his own, life changed for William Pryer during the 1880s, positively in terms of his marriage and negatively in terms of his professional life. He began to disagree with the strictly administrative character of company rule, which he saw as not interested enough in the economic potential which North Borneo represented for him and which had drawn Overbeck and Dent there in the first place. By the end of the 1880s he was convinced that the road to prosperity in North Borneo lay not in tariffs and taxes but in private agricultural development. Pryer actually resigned from his beloved company in 1890 and returned to England to interest people in his vision of North Borneo. He gathered investors who shared his enthusiastic views and became part of a newly formed company, the British North Borneo Development Corporation, and returned to North Borneo in 1891 committed to developing plantation crops.

The corporation was at least as undercapitalized as the company, and consequently suffered the same problems. The remainder of Pryer's years in Borneo continued to be a struggle to find investors, interspersed with great enthusiasm for his agricultural projects. He ran several plantations around Sandakan, full of optimism for his mangoes, his sugar, his hemp, his coconuts, his sago, and, most of all, his coffee. He ran tours of his estates for anyone he could persuade to come over from Singapore or Hong Kong or anywhere else, even interesting Dr Jose Rizal, the Philippine patriot and writer, in establishing a colony in North Borneo.[30] As his wife so succinctly put it in her diary, 'Willie's head [is] full of schemes', and his prayer is, 'may we get the coin'.[31]

In spite of Willie's schemes and prayers, the corporation failed. We hear that by January 1898 'all the money had been spent so that there are no funds left to go on with'(*Diary*, p. 95). Yet Pryer remained convinced of the possibility of progress, of what he had seen as 'great things for the country'(*Diary*, p. 33). But he had been working for those great things in North Borneo for twenty years, and was now in his fifties. He had health problems for several years. On 1 October 1898, after several months of severe illness, he and his wife set out for England on sick leave. Neither was to return. Ada's darling Willie died somewhere in the area of Port Said on 7 or 8 January 1899, two months short of his fifty-sixth birthday. The marriage had lasted a little over fifteen years. William was buried in Suez, and Ada retired to England. She was just 43. She settled in London, and died there seventeen years later on 12 February 1916, aged 60. She was buried near her parents in Maindee.

ADA'S LITTLE BOOK

In 1893, in the midst of William's struggles to generate the capital needed to make a commercial success of his plantations and fulfil his dreams about the glorious future of North Borneo, Ada published *A Decade in Borneo*. This little book was written at the service of those struggles and dreams. It has a unique role as the one book aimed at locating North Borneo for a general British audience. The book was to be literally a memoir of the early years of Ada's husband's pioneering activities and some aspects of their life together. A central purpose of the book was to ensure that the audience back home understood just what a hero William Pryer was and how far he had been personally and single-handedly responsible for the British successfully taking over British North Borneo, as well as recording what a wonderful place this region 'really' was. This was a crucial point, not simply because Ada adored her 'darling Willie' but because the willingness of investors to pledge capital to Willie's new development corporation depended a great deal on their perception of his achievements and the largeness of his reputation. That perception depended on distinguishing Willie's commercial commitment from Rajah Brooke's more fiery brand of imperialism, which scorned a profit motive. Would-be investors were betting on the man as well as the place. Moreover, not only private investors but also the British government had to be impressed. North Borneo's continuing political problem was how to successfully fend off the ongoing claims and aggressions of Rajah Charles Brooke, who was counting on the company's and corporation's financial failures in his relentless arguments to the Colonial Office that North Borneo should be turned over to Sarawak.

A *Decade in Borneo* thus functions on at least three levels: as a private and loving tribute, as a clarion call to private investors, and as an argument about the colonial status appropriate for British North Borneo. In the latter two senses, the book operates as a piece of economic and political propaganda which uses its feminine narrator as a useful way to join the debate about the British presence in Borneo as a matter of commercial development or romantic adventure. The implied logic is simple. To support commercial investment and development by British companies and individuals in British North Borneo can only mean to oppose the claims of Brooke, since the White Rajah was vividly on record as being opposed to the very concept of commercial development in Borneo.

The book begins with a little 'history' of the island which in its own way echoes a general British imperial attitude after the Napoleonic wars and throughout the nineteenth century. This 'history' teaches readers that the true enemies in Borneo, and the sources of greatest danger and destruction to almost anyone, have been other Europeans, particularly the French, the Dutch and the Spanish. Thus Pryer's entire opening chapter represents a Borneo which in the very 'Old Days' was prosperous and harmonious when left alone but which, with the advent of the bad Europeans, declined into poverty and piracy as local peoples were driven from their homes. Far from being anti-interventionist, this argument is not that Borneo and its peoples should be left alone again, but precisely that the British had to intervene and are the very nation that should be there. The peoples and lands of Borneo had already been decimated by England's enemies in Europe. Literally driven from their villages and dispersed, the people were forced to become homeless wanderers in their seas and their woods.

The general frame of the wickedness of previous European presences in contrast to the obligation and obliging nature of British occupation allows Ada to represent William's and her own presence in North Borneo as a gesture of friendship. It allows her to represent local resistance to William's takeover of large chunks of land and imposition of duties and taxes on local goods in the name of the BNBC in some very special ways. Not only is William not a pirate (which he might well be called by an anti-imperialist reader) but, just as important in this narrative, neither are the local resistant Malays 'really' pirates (which they were routinely called in British newspaper accounts). Piracy, in Ada Pryer's rhetorical lexicon, is a product of European corruption and thus vanishes when the right European, which is to say an Englishman such as her husband, appears. Local resistance to William Pryer's *de facto* rule and policies becomes represented as simply an early mistake, a learned and even appropriate response when facing the Spanish or the Dutch, but needing to be unlearned when dealing with William. In this account all the local Malays do unlearn their objections to being colonized as all become settlers, or resettlers, together.

North Borneo, in Pryer's memoir, is a kinder, gentler world, better than its own past, better than the neighbouring British colonial world of Sarawak, better even than England itself. William is initially presented as comparable to James Brooke of Sarawak, as just as heroic, a white man 'alone' in the jungle, conquering pirates, facing enormous odds, in order to carve out a harmonious state in a tropical paradise. Ada's readers must understand that William is just as great as the famous White Rajahs. In fact he is greater, because he is also presented as crucially different from Brooke, whose methods are to be understood as simply out of date. Those differences are marked in the narrative through gender, and serve to map the imperial geography of North Borneo as a potential money-making southern sister of British Malaya rather than a northern brother of Sarawak.

In the boys' adventure tales of the White Rajahs there was no place for women, any more than there was a place for Jewel in the Patusan of Conrad's *Lord Jim*. But in Pryer's memoir William is distinguished as a different kind of hero from James Brooke or Conrad's Tuan Jim. William makes friends rather than conquering enemies, and in the process reverses the cruel diaspora which was the legacy of a bad colonial past. Heroism in *A Decade in Borneo*, though about great physical courage, is not that all-too-familiar masculinity of adventure tales demonstrated by dashing through the jungle with weapons and waging battles. While there are a few references to fighting, the one incident which Ada actually recounts involving shooting is presented as a farce. William didn't use a gun but his police shot 412 cartridges, missed the fleeing Malays, hit the government boats five times by mistake, and ended up being fined (ch. 8).

In Chapters 2 to 4, which focus primarily on the narrative of William restoring peace to 'his' areas of North Borneo, the anecdotes Pryer narrates again and again construct a portrait of a hero with words, a guy who can talk, and who travels around in a small boat having successful chats. The emphasis is not on William's prowess but on his cleverness and charm. The repeated results are, in Pryer's language, that although there were 'moments of peril'(ch. 4) almost daily, they could be surmounted without violence. Instead of violence, 'by a little tact and judgment, and a firm stand, matters were arranged amicably'(ch. 3).

If William is portrayed as an amicable arranger, a man with a talent for persuasive talking rather than aggressive fighting, more feminine than masculine, the Malays are also presented as being full of a feminized sensitivity and charm. Since their resistance to William's takeover – strong at first and recurring in very occasional outbursts for several years – can be laid at the door of those other Europeans, it follows that the Malays themselves are pleased with the advent of William's and the BNBC's rule. The representation of masculinity as part of the old past with those 'other' Europeans and the representation of the Malays as participants in a new feminized present means that they are now all happy. The narrative is full of 'descriptions' of local peoples as gentle, charming, courteous, devoted, patient, and having the 'polished manners ... of civilization'(ch. 2), with tidy houses, pretty gardens, and villages offering a 'scene of contentment and plenty' (ch. 7).

A Decade in Borneo offers an economic geography in which North Borneo belongs with British Malaya rather than with Brooke's Sarawak. More specifically, in the rhetorical act of electing to sketch a landscape picture of imperialism which chooses business rather than adventure, Pryer radically modifies the masculinized iconography familiar to her imperial readers in those two choices. The narrator's claim is that North Borneo, and Southeast Asia more generally as represented by its great metropolitan centre of Singapore, is a superb place to do business because it is a superb place to live. Choosing business turns out to mean choosing not merely a profession but a way of life, and also choosing not gruelling work but delightful leisure. The narrator presents herself as having found the best of what we now call a 'lifestyle', full of nice things to do, with nice views and nice gardens, nice people to meet, nothing so 'enjoyable [as] a moonlight pic-nic on a large and comfortable steam launch' (ch. 12) and, as she emphasizes, 'snakes are quite scarce'(ch. 13). No mention of Willie's capture of 'a 20 foot python' here.

Pryer's narrative is a picture of the good life, one which images the product of doing business in North Borneo – graceful living in domestic companionship – rather than the process – those portraits of the heroic struggles of a lone individual, always male, always carrying a big knife, to carve something or other out of the wilderness. Her chapter on the steps involved in creating a coffee plantation, apparently about the process of creating a business, functions as an implicit argument for the lack of difficulty involved in that process. The text reads like a recipe for success, ten easy steps to making a coffee plantation. Pryer repeatedly praises the landscape of North Borneo, explicitly claiming that 'nowhere in England is there such lovely scenery'(ch. 5). In a more lengthy comparison, this time between England and Singapore, the narrator finds the better metropolitan location to be Singapore, 'a perfect paradise', with 'superb' roads as good as anything in England, without England's 'squalid and grimy poverty', with people of more buoyant spirits who are 'un-English' in ways that include their friendliness and 'hospitality'(ch. 11).

The comparisons with England function in *A Decade in Borneo* to emphasize that the narrative is a call for immigration and settlement, an argument that North Borneo is a wonderful place to live and call home. Specifically, it is a place where British women (those pretty views, that lack of snakes) would want to be. Colonization, in Pryer's narrative, is represented as about neither the hardships and enormous riches of tin mining and rubber planting nor the thrills of fighting pirates, about neither economics nor heroism. Certainly North Borneo offers profits, but imaged in a particular way. In the vision offered by this narrative, colonization is about graceful living, for women as much as for men, about fine, large, airy bungalows and creative cooks and beautiful scenery. It is about lovely moonlight parties and good roads. It is about the indigenous Malays as friends and neighbours, enjoying along with the Pryers the bounty and productivity brought by British rule, wishing along with the Pryers for more British families to settle and be part of the development of North Borneo, an event which can only increase the bounty and productivity of this beautiful world.

In this successful colonial present the place is peopled by willing though sparse settlers, both Malay and European, everybody busy making farms and businesses and villages and towns together. Both groups enjoy the same continuum of the good life, though one more simply and the other more elaborately. All they need is more people to join them in enjoying it too. The narrative's argument for immigration rejects portraits of North Borneo as a masculinized backdrop for a man's adventure tale – too much wilderness and danger required – and as a masculinized source of entrepreneurial business opportunities – too much individualism, and an unappetizing image of isolated mines and plantations.

Yet Pryer's feminized North Borneo, while emphatically communal, is not a private or interior domestic sphere. There are no children or family scenes here. Instead, *A Decade in Borneo* offers the feminized public sphere of the familiar bourgeois community: a heterosexual couple, concerned to have a nice house on good farmland, with solid business opportunities and a fulfilling social world. The book, ignoring such details as dense tropical rain forests with pathways navigated almost entirely by boat, invokes the rural pleasures of England's most beloved image of itself as a settled and productive agricultural land. These are precisely the values and images which Pryer invokes in her economic hymn to North Borneo. Her vision is that the greatness of England can live again, in the dream of a commercial future in this remote island world. She closes her narrative with the faith that 'the day cannot be far off ... when North Borneo's enormous capabilities must ... attract notice to this the finest tropical agricultural country that Great Britain possesses'.

Mecklenburg, New York, 1999

NOTES

1. This saying was quoted in reference to rubber in Malaya by an early-twentieth-century Director of the Royal Botanic Gardens. See Susan Morgan, *Place Matters: Gendered Geography in Victorian Women's Travel Books about Southeast Asia* (New Brunswick, NJ: Rutgers University Press, 1996), p. 148.
2. Quoted by K. G. Tregonning, *Under Chartered Company Rule (North Borneo 1881–1946)* (Singapore: University of Malaya Press, 1958), p. 25.
3. See *ibid.*, pp. 25–7.
4. I am indebted to Ian Black, *A Gambling Style of Government: The Establishment of the Chartered Company's Rule in Sabah, 1878–1915* (Kuala Lumpur: Oxford University Press, 1983), and L. R. Wright, *The Origins of British Borneo* (Hong Kong: Hong Kong University Press, 1970), for the following discussion, as well as to *Under Chartered Company Rule*.
5. Wright, *The Origins of British Borneo*, p. 8.
6. *Ibid.*, p. 1.
7. Nicholas Tarling, *The Burthen, the Risk, and the Glory: A Biography of Sir James Brooke* (Kuala Lumpur: Oxford University Press, 1982), pp. 125-31.
8. See esp. Nicholas Tarling's detailed analysis of the history of relations between the Brookes and the British government on the subject of the status of Sarawak in *Britain, the Brookes and Brunei* (Kuala Lumpur: Oxford University Press, 1971).
9. Colin N. Crisswell, *Rajah Charles Brooke: Monarch of All He Surveyed* (Kuala Lumpur: Oxford University Press, 1978), p. 57.
10. Quoted by Nicholas Tarling, *Britain, the Brookes and Brunei*, p. 56. Naval ships did help Brooke – sometimes simply by their presence and sometimes in actual battles – much more extensively than their orders allowed.
11. Quoted from Lord Derby by Emily Hahn, *James Brooke of Sarawak: A Biography of Sir James Brooke* (London: Arthur Barker, 1953), pp. 231–2.
12. Wright, *The Origins of British Borneo*, p. 202.
13. This information is provided by Ulla Wagner in her excellent account of Brooke rule, *Colonialism and Iban Warfare* (Stockholm: OBE-Tryck, 1972), p. 36.
14. Robert Pringle, *Rajahs and Rebels: The Ibans of Sarawak under Brooke Rule, 1841–1941* (Ithaca, NY: Cornell University Press, 1970), p. 120. I am indebted to Pringle's discussion of this incident (pp. 97–134).
15. *Ibid.*, p. 123.
16. Tarling, *Britain, the Brookes and Brunei*, p. 181.
17. Quoted by R. H. W. Reece, *The Name of Brooke: The End of White Rajah Rule in Sarawak* (Kuala Lumpur: Oxford University Press, 1982), p. 7.
18. Harriette McDougall, *Letters from Sarawak; Addressed to a Child* (Norwich: Thomas Priest, 1854), p. v. Further references are to this edition.

19. Robert Payne, *The White Rajahs of Sarawak* (1960; reprinted Singapore: Oxford University Press, 1986), pp. 14–15.

20. Reece, *The Name of Brooke*, p. xxv.

21. Review of *Memoirs of Francis Thomas McDougall, D.C.L., F.R.C.S., Sometime Bishop of Labuan and Sarawak, and of Harriette His Wife, Athenaeum*, no. 3244 (28 December 1889), p. 886.

22. Joseph Conrad, *Lord Jim* (1899; reprinted New York: New American Library, 1961), p. 307.

23. Reece, *The Name of Brooke*, p. xxv.

24. Tregonning, *Under Chartered Company Rule*, p. 41.

25. Black, *A Gambling Style of Government*, p. 23.

26. Quoted in Tregonning, *Under Chartered Company Rule*, p. 16.

27. Quoted by Wright, *The Origins of British Borneo*, p. 148.

28. Quoted by K. G. Tregonning, 'William Pryer, the Founder of Sandakan', *Journal of the Malayan Branch of the Royal Asiatic Society*, vol. 27 (1954), pp. 45–6.

29. L. S. von Donop, 'Diary of Mr. L. S. von Donop's Travels in Sabah in 1882', *Sabah Society Journal*, vol. 3 (March 1968), pp. 245–6.

30. Austin Coates, 'The Philippines National Hero: Rizal in Sandakan', *Sarawak Museum Journal*, vol. 10 (July–December, 1962), pp. 537-53.

31. Nicholas Tarling (ed.), *Mrs. Pryer in Sabah: Diaries and Papers from the Late Nineteenth Century* (Auckland: University of Auckland, 1989), pp. 43, 58. Hereafter referred to as *Diary*.

NOTE ON THE TEXT

A Decade in Borneo was originally published in 1893 by Kelly and Walsh of Hong Kong, Shanghai, Yokohama and Singapore, and by Hutchinson of London in 1894. The text was the same in both, but the cover and paper were different. Ada Pryer was disappointed in the cover and paper of the Hong Kong edition, as well as with the printing errors in both. This book is a reprint of the original Hutchinson edition, with what are obviously printing errors corrected.

Ada Pryer did want to publish a second edition, which not only corrected printing errors but, more significantly, offered major additions to the chapters. Working with some help from William, who had also offered minor contributions and corrections to the first edition, Ada produced a draft of a significantly enlarged second edition. It was never published, but the draft was preserved. A copy now exists, along with Ada Pryer's diary, among the North Borneo Company records in the Public Record Office in London. The draft of the second edition additions and much of the diary is also available in print, as *Mrs. Pryer in Sabah*, edited and with an introduction by Nicholas Tarling, printed by the Centre for Asian Studies, University of Auckland, 1989.

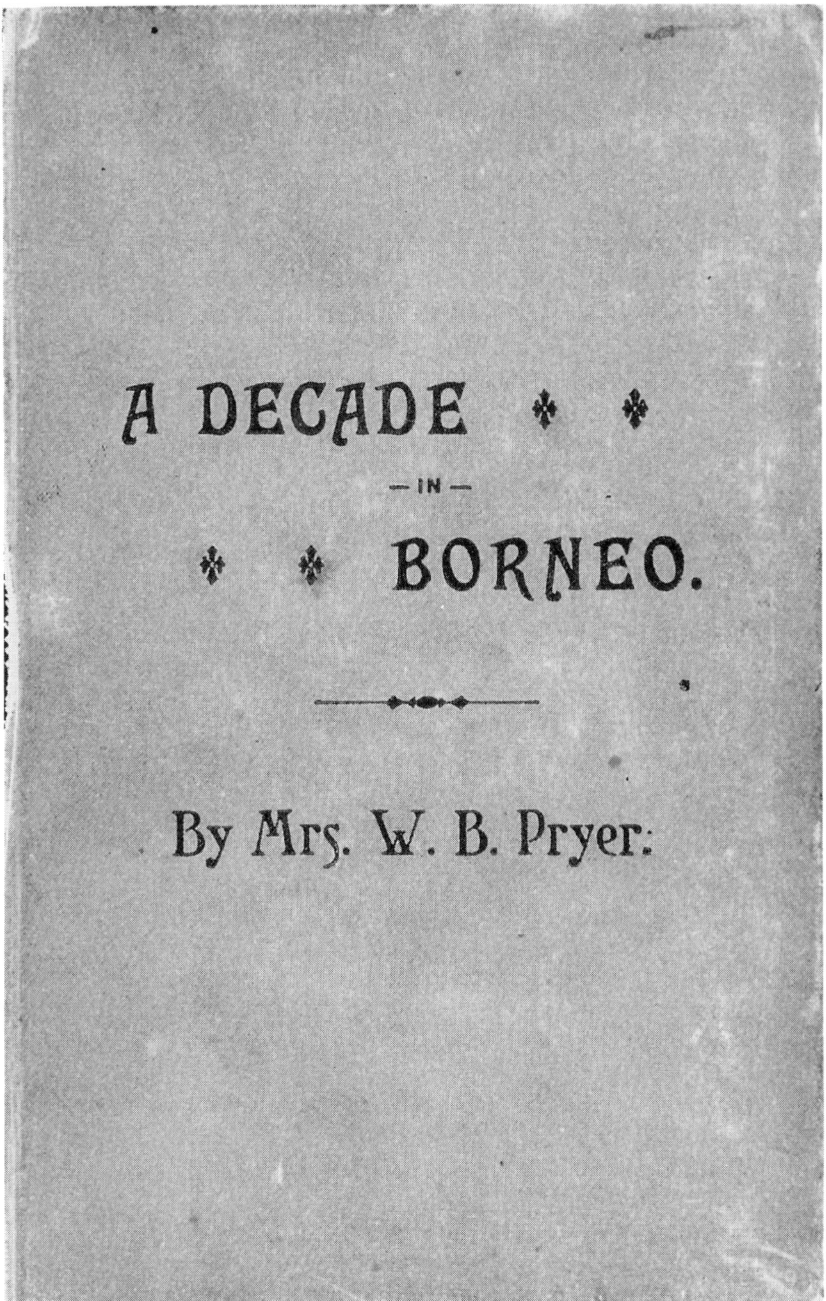

A DECADE ✦ ✦

— IN —

✦ ✦ BORNEO.

By Mrs. W. B. Pryer:

Plate 1 Cover of original edition of *A Decade in Borneo*, Kelly & Walsh Ltd, Hongkong, Shanghai, Yokohama and Singapore, 1893.

Preface.

This little book does not presume to give more than a bare outside of the events connected with the acquisition of North Borneo and the matters that led up to the formation of the British North Borneo Company, beyond which point I do not think the time has yet arrived when it is advisable to continue the history.

I here take the opportunity of offering my thanks to Mr. HORACE Cox, proprietor of "The Field," for his courtesy in allowing me to reproduce certain papers which originally appeared in the columns of his paper.

I pen this preface in a clearing in the heart of the Bornean forest, whilst all the varied work in connection with the opening of a large Coffee and Manila-Hemp Estate is in full operation, and I sincerely venture to hope that this little book may at least have the effect of attracting greater interest and attention to the unrivalled agricultural advantages of this fertile land.

ADA PRYER.

KABELI RIVER MEADE ESTATE
18th January, 1893.

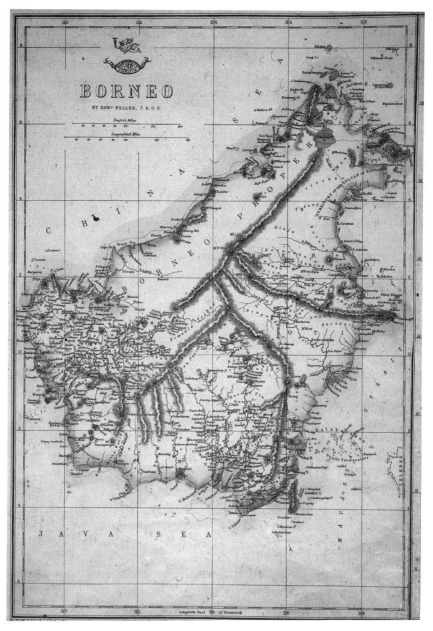

Plate 2   Edward Weller, 'Borneo', *Weekly Dispatch Atlas*, 1880.
Source: National Library of Australia, Canberra.

INTRODUCTION.

The names of Pryer and British North Borneo are in my mind almost synonymous.

When some years ago I sat down under the inspiration of Sir Alfred Dent to write the first book upon the new Company of exploration and settlement which was published under the title of "The New Ceylon" the travel notes and experiences of Mr. W. B. Pryer were among the most valuable documents with which I had to deal.[1] Captain Witti's diaries were intensely interesting. The Austrian officer looked at things from the traveller's points of view, with here and there a suggestion of commercial possibilities thrown in; but Mr. Pryer's diaries never for a moment lost sight of the business side of the great Borneo question. Planting, mining, the cultivation of this, and the mercantile value of the other were foremost considerations with him, coupled with the condition of tribes and races in so far as they might be amenable to civilizing influences and become factors in the peaceful and commercial development of the country.

The first white resident in the territories of the British North Borneo Company and one of its most enthusiastic officers, Mr. Pryer, in taking up an independent position in the country as he now has done, should be able the better to advance its interests. His faith in the future has long been established by his making North Borneo his home, and his wife is none the less earnest than himself in the work of realizing their unbounded faith in one of the most patriotic of modern enterprises.

Mrs. Pryer in the following pages has added much to our knowledge of Borneo, and she keeps well in view the main objects of the founders of the latest British possession. I feel honoured in being asked to write a few lines by way of Preface to a work which so happily combines utility with romance, and constitutes a new and stirring chapter in the history of the Eastern Seas.

My feeling for Borneo is more or less sentimental, but it begins with the first great efforts of London to plant there a British Colony, a new national possession; and my heart goes out to a bit of jungle, near Elopura, where a new cemetery bears witness to the heroism of men and women who have contributed their lives to the new state.

It is a piece of great good fortune that Mr. Pryer has been spared to put the finishing touches to many schemes, to drive home some of the ambitious hopes of dead and gone colleagues who had caught his own faith and the belief of such authorities as Sir Alfred Dent, Sir Rutherford Alcock, Mr. R. Biddulph Martin, Baron Overbeck, Mr. W. M. Crocker and others in the future of North Borneo as a competitor for the sale of tropical products in the great markets of the world.

JOSEPH HATTON.

GARRICK CLUB, LONDON
1893.

CONTENTS.

CHAPTER IV.
ELOPURA.

CHAPTER V.
BIRDSNESTING, AND A HUNT IN BORNEO.

CHAPTER VI.
UP THE RIVER KINABATANGAN.

CHAPTER VII.
UP THE RIVER KINABATANGAN.—(CONTINUED).

CHAPTER VIII.
AMONG BULUDUPIES AND BAJOWS.

CHAPTER IX.
SOOLOO AND THE SOOLOOS.

CHAPTER X.
MALAYS.

CHAPTER XI.
SINGAPORE TO SANDAKAN.

CHAPTER XII.
SANDAKAN.

CHAPTER XIII.
MISCELLANEOUS.

CHAPTER XIV.
COFFEE PLANTING.

CHAPTER XV.
CONCLUSION.

A Decade in Borneo.

Chapter I.
General and Introductory.

Borneo.—Size and position of.—How divided.—Early history.—Piggafetta.—Beeckman.—Pepper contracts.—Pirates and head-hunters.—Depredation of.—Population destroyed by.—Extracts from Dalton, Carl Bock, Witti, and Spencer St. John.—Desperate state of affairs in 1876.

Borneo is such a far away island and so much a terra incognita to the general British public, that, without suggesting in any way a lack of geographical or other knowledge on the part of the reader, I venture to preface the account of my experiences in this remote part of the world by giving a short sketch of its position and early history, especially as there are not many authorities who afford much reliable information on the subject, and such books as do exist are principally from the pens of long passed away travellers and are therefore somewhat difficult to obtain.

Borneo is the largest island in the world, being about 820 miles from North to South, and 600 in its greatest breadth. It lies to the East of the Straits Settlements, having Java and Australia to the South, the Philippines and China to the North, and Celebes and the Moluccas to the East. It extends from 7.30° N. to 4° S., the equator thus, it will be seen, runs through the centre of the island. By way of comparison I may mention that it is rather more than three times the size of Great Britain and contains an area of 280,000 square miles.

It is divided as follows:– the greater portion of the island southwards is claimed by the Dutch; to the West lies Sarawak, ruled over by Rajah Brooke; above his territory is situated an independent native state, the Sultanate of Brunei; whilst the northern part of the island constitutes the British Protected State of North Borneo, and ranks in size 11th on the list of all England's colonies. The little island of Labuan lies off Brunei. The native name of the whole island is Pulo Kalamantan.

The whole of Borneo may be roughly spoken of as one vast virgin forest, intersected by large rivers. The greater portion of the land to the South is flat and probably not very healthy; further northward it becomes more hilly, culminating in the grand mountain of Kina Balu, 13,700 ft. high. North Borneo is the most interesting and picturesque, as also the most healthy portion, of the whole island.

Though it has never at any time been thickly populated, when it was first discovered by Europeans there were a great many more people in the island than is the case at present: a fairly strong government maintained passable order, a large trade existed with China, and Chinese immigration was in full swing. Pepper gardens abounded in various parts and matters generally were in a sufficiently prosperous state.

Piggafetta, who visited Brunei, the capital, so long ago as 1521, gave a particular and very interesting account of his stay there, from which we gather that the town then contained many thousands of houses: gaily caparisoned elephants walked through its solid streets; affairs of state were administered in a proper way; trade and agriculture were in progress; and there was every evidence that authority was maintained and lawlessness repressed.[2]

For the next 200 years, or thereabouts, things went on much in the same way, and Captain Beeckman, who visited the Banjer-massing district in 1716, found the country ruled by Sultans in a strong if somewhat high-handed manner: the junk trade with China was well maintained, and the country tolerably thickly inhabited.[3] He was able at once to make a contract for the delivery of from 500,000 to 700,000 lbs. of pepper at one single place, at the low price of about 3d per lb., which affords a good indication of the extent of the trade then existing, as well as of the size of the rural population.

During the next hundred years a change came over the state of affairs. The influence of Europeans, Spanish, Portuguese, and Dutch, gradually extended. The arrogant and grasping native Sultans and Rajahs came face to face with people as arrogant and grasping as themselves, but with more power. Monopolies were declared and enforced; trade was restricted; the junk trade with China put an end to, the revenues of the native princes curtailed, or stopped altogether; their authority upset, and themselves driven to desperation in various ways; and as little or no attempt was made, in Borneo, at least, to substitute any other government for those destroyed, everyone struggled for his own hand, and chaos supervened.

About the beginning of the present century all the powers of evil seemed let loose to do their worst in the beautiful and fertile land on a scale rarely witnessed in the world's history.[4] Pirate flotillas continually swept the coast, not confining themselves to operations at sea simply, but burning and plundering villages and placing whole districts under contribution; the endeavours of the Dutch to enforce taxation were the cause of devastating wars, particularly against the Chinese, who, to the number of some quarter of a million, then inhabited the West coast of Borneo. The Dyaks of the interior freely, and without restraint, indulged their passion for head-hunting, and even put to sea in large fleets for the purpose of ascending neighbouring rivers to conduct their massacres on a wholesale scale; human sacrifice (bought slaves being usually the victims) was frequent nearly everywhere,* the native Rajahs endeavoured to make up their decreasing revenues by increasing their extortions; the dreaded Illanuns, goaded to desperation by the Spaniards, swept the seas from Manila on the North, to Batavia on the South, attacking, plundering, and murdering all they met, as many, even of our own merchantmen, found to their cost;** the less manly, but not less ferocious, Balignini crept everywhere along the coast and amongst the islands kidnapping people at night, even in the Bay of Manila itself.***

From various authorities, dating from the early years of the century, we gather such statements as the following:

> It is a deplorable fact that within the last ten or twelve years piracy has, in various parts of this archipelago, increased in a frightful manner, it has now become a trade and is carried on systematically by the principal Bugis Rajahs.

---

*   Of 4,000 persons kidnapped amongst the Sooloo Islands, as late as the year 1878, and sold in the Sambakong river, it was estimated that fully one half were thus murdered.

**   One pirate chief alone had four European women, who had been captured from vessels, in his house at one time.

***   The following is a list of depredations committed by Illanuns alone, in the six months of the year 1814: "One Spanish brig from Manila; 20 smaller craft captured amongst the Philippines; 1,000 people kidnapped from the Spanish Islands and sold as slaves; one large boat from Macassar; five or six smaller craft, under English colours; the boat's crew of an English brig; and the watering party of H. M. S. *Fox* – in all 25 Europeans." As recently as 1872 when W. was travelling in the Philippines, three villages in the same island he was on were attacked at night by Balignini, and partly burned, and several persons, principally young women, carried off during the confusion.

In November, 1827, a chief of pirates, named Sindow, made a descent upon Mamoodgo with 45 prahus, burned three-quarters of a kampong, some scores of men were killed, and 300 made prisoners, besides women and children. During my stay there, ten weeks, the place was visited by two other pirate chiefs; between them they had 134 prahus of all sizes: the Kylie Rajah, who first arrived, fired into the kampong night and day. Of Mamoodgo the people are estimated at 35,000; Markammar contains about 3,000 inhabitants, and there are here, at Marpow, 106 Dyak Rajahs, each having from 300 to 1,000 men. – *Dalton's Papers on Borneo.**

With regard to the head-hunters we read:

The Rajah of the country, Wagoo, has 70 chiefs under him, Sedgen has 50, while Selgie has more than 140. He calculates the people under his sway at 150,000. The ravages of these people are dreadful. In August, 1828, Selgie returned from an expedition, his party had been three weeks absent, during which time, besides detached houses, he had destroyed 17 kampongs (villages) with the whole of the men and old women, the young women and children were brought prisoners. No Dyak can marry unless he has previously taken a head or two. The burial places are encircled with strong bamboos upon which fresh heads are placed. From the last excursion Selgie's people brought with them 700 heads. – *Dyaks of Borneo*, Dalton, 1831.[5]

Extracts such as these from contemporary authorities could be multiplied indefinitely. With all these causes operating no wonder the population rapidly decreased, but not so rapidly but that years after this we find "the population on the coast of these large islands – Borneo (East Coast) and Celebes – was immense," while that of North Borneo was spoken of as large. From Malludu to Sibuco and beyond there were said to be tens of thousands of people, but this district and particularly the Sibuco part of it, by 1860, had not only virtually, but absolutely, become depopulated; still, however, there were a good many people left in the Paitan, Sugut, and neighbouring districts, as Spencer St. John testifies.[6] Most of these have since disappeared. In the year 1840 a gleam of hope appeared on the South-West Coast, where Sir James Brooke interposed between the native Dyaks and their Brunei oppressors; stopped the wars

---

*   All these statements refer to quite another part of the island to where the Illanun depredations already mentioned took place.

and massacres then in progress; took over the government of the Sarawak district, and established peace and order within his boundaries; thus accomplishing one of the finest, if not the finest, work ever undertaken by one individual man.[7] Everyone has, I suppose, read of the tough but triumphant struggles he had with the Malay Rajahs, the Seribas and Sekarran Dyaks, wholesale murderers (now two of the most obedient and tractable tribes), and finally with the Illanun pirates. The present Rajah, Sir Charles Brooke, has worthily followed the footsteps of his great predecessor, carrying the reign of law and order further and further into the land.

The following extracts from Carl Bock and Witti, show the state of affairs existing up to virtually the present time: –

"Births and namings, marriages and burials, cannot be properly celebrated unless the heads of a few enemies, more or less, have been secured. It is a rule, among all the tribes, that no youth can regularly wear a weapon, or be married, or associate with the opposite sex, till he has been on one or more head-hunting expeditions. Head-hunting is the keystone in the edifice of Dyak religion and character, its perpetual practice is no doubt one great cause of the rapid extinction of the race. At a trivah feast not only are the captives who have been taken prisoners sacrificed, but the richer members of the community give a number of slave-debtors to be put to death. Mr. Perelaer describes a trivah at which 40 slave-debtors were slaughtered." – Vide Carl Bock's "Head-hunters of Borneo."[8]

"The two adjacent districts of Nabai and Peluan have a feud; killed by Nabai 16 people, 10 per contra Peluan – page 16. I said they could no longer receive a slave for the purpose of sacrificing her in amends for the murder of Ah Hook, a Chinaman – page 16. Ankaroi complained that Jeludin and party carried off his wife and two little children, girls, and put them all three to death in the cruel manner called ambirno – page 23. The interview would have left no unpleasant impression on my mind if I had not seen a human hand and forearm, perhaps a fortnight old, nailed up on a door-post – page 26. And so on *ad lib.*" – Vide *Witti's last Expedition.*[9]

The Northern part of Borneo generally had been gradually but steadily deteriorating, the acreage of cultivated land had become less and less: on the East Coast, Sooloo Datos; on the West Coast, Brunei Pangerans wrung a large proportion of what crops were raised from the unfortunate people; irruptions of head-hunters destroyed individuals, parties, and even from time to time whole villages; no boat dared to go to sea without being fully equipped and manned for a struggle with pirates. The decreasing population was so harassed and driven from place to place that no permanent cultivation of the soil was possible. Brunei itself degenerated

Plate 3 G. McCulloch, 'The Sea Dyaks', lithograph, from Spenser St John, *Life in the Forests of the Far East: Travels in Sabah and Sarawak in the 1860s*, London, 1873. *Source:* National Library of Australia, Canberra.

into being nothing better than a town of tumbledown mat-sheds, standing on rotting poles over the water, the streets being wood-work erections above the river, in a dilapidated condition, while the Sultan's house itself was but a large old barn; the whole being a sad contrast to the prosperity and state which existed 450 years before.

In the year 1876, matters on the N.E. Coast were about as bad as they could be.

The rivers Paitan, Labuk, Sugut, and Kinabatangan, had to be ascended for a distance of sixty miles before the first villages were arrived at; whilst the rivers Moanud, Blocking, Segama and Sibuco, all of which had once been well populated, had not a single inhabitant left! Outside Sandakan Bay four villages only existed on the whole shore line, three of them inhabited by men of doubtful character, and freely resorted to by pirates, whose ranks they frequently augmented; whilst the fourth, Tuncu, was a pirate village pure and simple, under the charge of the famous Illanun chief, Dato Kurunding, a man who used to show a barong with which he boasted he had taken 120 lives. The birds' nest caves of Gomanton in the one direction, and of Madai and Segaloong, in the other, caused the existence of two small trading communities, always under the protection of powerful Sooloo Datos, notwithstanding which, however, they were usually attacked, by some one or other, every two or three years. During this year, it was computed, that 400 persons had been either murdered or captured by the pirates along the coast.

Sandakan Bay, the only place in which there were Chinese trading shops, had been raided twice; once, by head-hunters from the South, who took, amongst others, the head of the second most powerful Bajau chief of those parts, and once by Balignini; and the whole country was one forest of millions of acres, in which there existed, all told, but ten villages; most of them built on piles over the water, with scarcely a tree at their backs felled: roads or paths there were absolutely none, with the exception of two tracks, one to the Gomanton birds' nest caves, and the other to those of Madai in Darvel Bay. All rice was imported, and was bartered in exchange for forest and sea produce, at prices never less than $6 or $7 a picul, and occasionally as high as $20. Every man moved about armed, and blood was spilt on the slightest provocation.

Such was Borneo in the Old Days, but a new era was about to commence – the history of which I will now proceed to narrate.

Plate 4 T. Ficken, 'The City of Brunei – Sunset', lithograph, from Spenser St John, *Life in the Forests of the Far East: Travels in Sabah and Sarawak in the 1860s*, London, 1873.
Source: National Library of Australia, Canberra.

Chapter II.
Starting the Colony.

Fitting out the expedition.—Its members.—The "America."—
Obtaining the Brunei and Sooloo concessions.—War between
Spaniards and Sooloos.—Pearls.—Installation of W. at
Sandakan.—Dent's house flag adopted.—Sandakan, its trade,
&c.—The first act of administration.—Notification I.—W. to be
burnt out.—Emaum Jelanee.—Skirmish with head-hunters.—
Establishing law and order.—Mahomedan civilization.—
Administering Nakoda Meyer's estate.—Anderson sees the
devil.—Birdsnest caves.—Pangeran Sama, atrocities by.—
Expedition against.—The Kina Batangan opened to trade.

During the early part of the seventies, the fertility of the soil and the
fineness of the climate had attracted attention, and one or two bona fide
attempts to establish a better state of affairs in the country had been
made, with varying success, but at last a properly organized expedition
was fitted out, in 1877, by Mr. Alfred Dent (now Sir Alfred Dent,
K.C.M.G.) which was under the immediate command of Baron Overbeck,
who left England with a staff of two or three, of whom my husband was
one, to see what could be effected.[10]

The journey to Singapore was uneventful, but in November the party –
consisting of the Baron; Mr. Prettyman; my husband, W. B. Pryer; with
Mr. Torry, U.S. Consul at Bangkok – left that port on their adventurous
voyage in the steamer "America," specially chartered and fitted up for the
expedition.

All the preparations were conducted with great secrecy, but the
suspicions of the Dutch and Spanish consuls were aroused, and the
smallest movements in connection with the "America" were keenly
watched, telescopes being brought to bear upon her as she lay in the
harbour making ready. Sundry applications to try to prevent her starting,
in which the word "Buccaneer" was freely used, were made to the
authorities, but without avail, and the alarm of the several consuls was
not diminished by the fact of her steaming alongside the powder hulk and
taking on board a large supply of ammunition. This alarm was not
confined to the people on shore alone, as, next morning, when well out to
sea, the staff of Chinese servants, on seeing the hold opened and various
guns and cannon brought on deck, went to the captain in a body and
demanded to be put on shore at once, although the nearest land was by
that time 100 miles away.

At Brunei, after considerable difficulty, the treaty of 29th December,

1877, was obtained: it was a matter of touch and go whether they were likely to get it or not, for after several days spent in fruitless negociations, the "America" was ordered down the river, and the steam launch was lying, with steam up, ready to follow her, whilst a last effort was being made to conclude the matter satisfactorily; at this critical moment H.M.S. "Hart" was unexpectedly seen steaming up the river.

Before she rounded into Brunei, however, the negociations, had, at last, been successfully accomplished, and the papers had just been signed and sealed a few moments previously; otherwise, matters might have been much prolonged, and even, perhaps, broken off altogether. The treaty having been successfully arranged at Brunei, the "America" got up steam and, after touching at Labuan, where the party was augmented by Mr. Cowie, started for Sooloo, accompanied by H.M.S. "Hart," with the Consul-General for Borneo on board.[11] Upon arriving at Sooloo it was found that the Spaniards were making war upon the Sooloos, in connection with which a fortunate set of incidents to which, however, I cannot at present allude, helped forward the negociations.

The war that was then being waged in Sooloo presented some curious features, over a thousand Spanish troops, in addition to a fleet in the roads, were cooped up behind the walls of the little city by a much inferior native force. The actual siege was conducted by eight men who had, between them, four rifles; four men mounting guard over the city full of Spaniards, whilst the other four slept and ate. The party of Englishmen were able to move about the island at will, whereas had they been Spanish they would have been amooked by the first Sooloo they met.

During this visit the Sultan gave a dinner, at which the plates used were huge pearl oyster shells with pearls to the value of several hundred dollars embedded in them.

Having arranged matters in Sooloo, thus settling the cross claims of both the Sultan of Sooloo and Brunei, the "America" steamed across to Sandakan, where my husband was duly installed as the Governor of the N.E. Coast, receiving his commission (which was as Resident only, however) from Baron Overbeck, and, on the 11th of February, 1878, the "America" again hauled up her anchor and left him in charge; his entire staff for the inauguration of law and order, along a coast line of 300 miles, infested by pirates and marauders of the worst type, being a West Indian black named Anderson, a half-caste Hindoo named Abdul, and a couple of China boys. For provisions they had a barrel of flower and 17 fowls; the artillery consisted of half a dozen Snider rifles.

The flag adopted was the old Paou Shun (Dent & Co.'s house flag).

At this time, the entire population of Sandakan Bay consisted of the inhabitants of three villages hidden away in one of the numerous side arms of the Bay, screened by mangroves – a spot specially selected on account of its being difficult to find without a guide – chosen for the sake of concealment, as it had been a blockade running depot by a foreign firm who used to run their cargoes across to Sooloo from there. The place had not long before been attacked by head-hunters, and a fierce battle had also been fought by its inhabitants against a fleet of pirates from the South. One of the villages, Oopak, was inhabited by a considerable number of Bajaus (sea-gipsy tribe); the second, Timbong, was the head-quarters of a trading Sooloo, Dato Hadji Mohamed Ansurudeen; and the third, Sandakan proper, although it only contained 17 houses, was the centre of trade of the whole district. Its population was a mixed one, comprising, Chinese, Arab, Malay and Sooloo traders, while the amount of business done was somewhat out of proportion to the size of the place, as what jungle produce was permitted to be brought out of the rivers Kinabatangan and Labuk, as well as the Lincabo seed-pearls and the Gomanton birds' nests (edible), mostly passed through the hands of its traders.

W.'s first act of administration was the issuing of regulations imposing duties upon all trade passing through the port,* and I may say that from

---

* The following has an interest as being a copy of the first notification ever issued in North Borneo, marking the commencement of a new order of things in the country:

CUSTOMS DEPARTMENT
Notification 1.

All vessels arriving here from Foreign Ports will pay Tonnage dues as under–
      Vessels under 200 tons....................$ 5
      Vessels over 200 tons.....................$10

All foreign goods arriving will pay import duty 4 per cent, after which they are subject to no further charge.

All goods, the produce of the country, will pay, when exported, 4 per cent.

All foreign goods landed at Sandakan and re-exported will pay a duty of 1 per cent.

No duty is chargeable on goods not landed although they may be transhipped from vessel to vessel in harbour provided they are re-exported to foreign ports.

All vessels arriving here from foreign ports must hand in a manifest of their cargo to the Custom House and no cargo is to be delivered without a permit from the Resident.

that day to this a customs' tariff has been systematically enforced. At this step there was naturally some dissatisfaction expressed amongst the population, at first, but W. called together the head men, pointed out to them that they had been hitherto exposed to extortions and plunder at the hands of all outsiders, whereas, if they all worked together under him, they could defy intruders; the traders had had to give long credit; sometimes when they ascended the rivers to collect their debts they were plundered and illtreated; while the Bajaus and others were oppressed by Sooloo chiefs who sold them goods at impossible prices, demanding instant payment, sometimes seizing them as slaves in default, while all were alike subject to attack by pirates, head-hunters, and freebooters generally, and, in fact, every person's hand was against everybody elses: and that all this had to be put right. The Bajaus did not at all fall in with this idea at first, but held two meetings at which the advisability of burning W. out was freely discussed. Their head chief, Emaum Jelanee, being absent at the time, a boat was sent for him in order to bring him back, that his advice might be heard before any serious steps were taken.

Before his arrival, however, an event happened which tended very much to throw the position into W.'s hands. A boat came in hurriedly from Timbong, after nightfall, reporting that the village was being attacked by head-hunters. W. instantly called together the men of Sandakan and, after assigning to them the positions they were to occupy behind the stockade erected in the rear of the village, on purpose to meet such a possibility, he took some of the men he could place most reliance upon and went off with them to the assistance of Timbong. There he found everything in great confusion, a little skirmish had taken place, the stockade was lined with armed men, whilst the women were hurriedly pitching their goods and chattels into boats. W. made a short expedition into the surrounding country, but without seeing anyone, the marauders having retreated into the forest, and after returning and reassuring the people by his presence for sometime, he left them some of his men and, with the balance, rowed back to Sandakan, from whence he, at once, sent

cont.

> All native boats and prahus of whatever size with any cargo on board, however little, arriving from any place, must hand in a list of their cargo, although it may not be subject to duty.

Sandakan, 11th February, 1878

W.B. Pryer,
Resident

a boat across to Oopak, commanding the chief there, Panglima Abdul Rahman, to come across with a hundred of his men next day to assist in fighting the head-hunters, their mutual enemies.

Next morning, accordingly, there was a general assembly; the Bajaus, under the charge of a Mr. Martin, who was in charge of a trading store, were sent round up another arm of the sea and told to line the shore at the back of Timbong; whilst W., with a force of Sooloos, Buludupies and Malays, marched across from Timbong Island. The enemy had occupied some huts in the centre of the island, but fled, and the effort to drive them into the Bajau lines was unsuccessful, but the main result of the whole affair was that everyone had become accustomed to be ordered about by W. and matters ran along much more easily afterwards.

Tuan Emaum, the Bajou chief, returning a day or two later, W. sent for him, and pointed out to him that at present the people, disunited, were at the mercy of everybody who attacked or oppressed them; whereas, united, they need not fear anyone, and might order and enforce a better state of things everywhere within striking distance of Sandakan. The Emaum was a little scared at first, but finally consented to throw in his lot with him, and from that time his men, up to 250 in number, were always ready whenever required by W.

The next step was to establish a Court of Justice. W. at first had some difficulty in making the head-men understand that British justice was irrespective of person, and that all men were equal before it, but he firmly insisted upon his decisions being carried into effect and, although there was some grumbling and discontent, the voice of general opinion was behind him, and people sooner got into the way of obeying his judgments than might have been supposed.

The following extract from W.'s diary gives a glimpse into the home-life of the people:

March 24th, 1878, Sunday. Visited Nacoda Meyer at Oopak, he appears very ill and seems likely to die, he has a large house and is apparently the richest man in the harbour. His part of a large and airy house is partitioned off with scarlet hangings, the floor is well matted and strewn with pillows covered with red-figured silk. Hadji Omar, Panglima Abdul Rahman, and one or two other Hadjis and Nacodas, were there, dressed in bright-coloured silks, with handsome creeses, &c., and while we were there, a prahu, which had that morning arrived from Palawan, sailed over from Sandakan with two more Hadjis and a Nacoda. Chocolate, with small cakes, was served on good dishes, and as I noticed the bright and handsome arrangements of the room, the dignified but determined carriage of the men all accustomed to face danger, the cleanliness of everything, and the grave and polished manners of the guests, all betokening civilization, I could not but think more favourably of Mohammedanism.

There was no monotony, however, in the daily life, and the above-mentioned civilization did not prevent the men from crimes of violence: three following paragraphs in W.'s diary refer, one, to a murder up country; one to a trial of thieves; and one to a possible attack on the village itself.

The most serious affair which happened about this period, beginning of April, 1878, came about in connection with the above-mentioned Nacoda Meyer's estate. He having died a day or so after W. visited him, his brother Nacoda Ah Hung, thereupon loaded a lot of his dead brother's goods into a prahu, proposing to sail away to Sooloo with all these goods and thus defraud the creditors. Hearing of this, W. sent and told him to come over to attend a meeting of those interested: but Ah Hung sent answer that if he did come it would be with 50 men armed with creeses. This defiant attitude could not be allowed to pass, or else W.'s authority would have ended, so, in the middle of that night, without any previous warning, W. called out a lot of men, including some of the traders who were creditors, and he and his party paddled across the Bay in three or four prahus, quietly landed at Ah Hung's house, and suddenly rushing into the room, told his men to "order arms" alongside the Nacoda's bed. The prahu was then seized and taken across to Sandakan with all the goods for adjudication.

The Nacoda tried to pay a return visit the next night and had very nearly got his boat under the mat-shed W. was living in (which was built on poles over the sea) with the intention of setting it on fire, but was seen in time and prevented from carrying his intention into effect.

Ludicrous incidents sometimes occurred. On one occasion Anderson saw the devil. The following is an account of the interview; it was about 9 o'clock:

He had been talking to Nakoda Gumbah's son and to Ulass, at the end of the jetty, and then strolled up the jetty past his own door towards the Chinaman's, Chen Ko's, at the door of the godown in front; there on the jetty was the devil; at first he appeared like a rather strange dog, but, while he looked at him, his colour changed from white to black and he increased largely in size and his eyes became like blazing lamps. Anderson was afraid and fled to the house, where he told Chang Lock, who refused to come out, so he took a pistol and returned alone, there was the devil still, but in the guise now of a man or something like one, with his face turned the wrong way and his eyes like flaming lamps. Anderson aimed at it but the pistol refused to go off, and Anderson felt his hair rising on his head so that it lifted his cap off (rather a difficult accomplishment considering his close woolly crop); the devil made as though it was coming towards him and he made the sign of the cross on the ground, repeated a prayer, and retreated backwards with his face towards it until out of its sight. Meeting some one on the jetty, he returned again, but there was nothing there only a bad smell. He then came into my house, in an utterly unnerved condition.

There was plenty to keep W. occupied, the main object was, of course, to get the district into something like order and discipline, and after that to extend his influence to more distant parts of the territory; but, besides that, in addition to holding courts, interviewing native head-men and so forth, there was the necessity of keeping all the accounts of the station and customs, and issuing such notifications from time to time as tended to the establishment of law and order, besides reporting fully upon all matters to England. As soon as matters in Sandakan Bay had been brought into a somewhat better state, W. began to appreciate the necessity of turning his attention to bettering the condition of things elsewhere.

The first matter to claim attention was clearly the necessity of opening to trade the Kinabatangan. This river, the most important in British North Borneo, has its origin in the far interior, vague rumours of the importance of the district, its large population and wealth, reached W.'s ears from time to time. Edible birds' nest caves of reputed great value were said to exist at several places, large districts were said to be under cultivation and the forest to be full of natural products. It was, at all events, certain that one birds' nest cave, possessing many thousands of dollars' worth of nests, existed, as large quantities of these nests passed through Sandakan, in the course of trade. The river had to be ascended some 60 miles before the first villages were reached; these villages were under the dominance of a certain chief, Pangeran Sama by name, a man of very bad character, determined and cruel, who levied heavy taxes on all goers and comers, and sought to bring the natives of the higher river under his sway. From time to time rumours of the atrocities he committed reached W. and when he sent up to demand the amount of tribute nests due to the Sultan of Sooloo, but now transferred to the association which W. represented, he returned an insolent reply and immediately adopted an arrogant demeanour towards the Sandakan traders then in his village, culminating in his plundering and illtreating two of them, seizing all their goods, and leaving one of them for dead. The other promptly come down to Sandakan and reported the matter to W., who at once appreciated the fact that, if he was to have command of the country, this man must without delay be dealt with; so he gathered together a flotilla composed of Bajaus, Sooloos, Malays, Bugis and even Arab traders, and with this polyglot force proceeded up the river to the head-quarters of Pangeran Sama, Melapi.

It took five days to ascend the river, but at last Melapi was reached. Dato Hadji Ansurudeen's house, to which W. was bound, was above that of Pangeran Sama's, and as the Pangeran had a whole lot of small cannon pointing from some stockaded forts over the river, and had threatened to blow W. to pieces as he rowed by, and went about with two creeses in his sash to keep his men up to the mark, W. felt somewhat uncomfortable as he passed, expecting a volley every minute. However, he was allowed to go by without molestation, and safely reached the Dato's house, from whence he sent orders for the Pangeran to come to him; as he did not comply W. finally sent him notice that, unless he personally made his submission in three days, he would be attacked. The Pangeran made a great show of arming his men, fully 500 in number, but of inferior physique to the brawny Bajaus who accompanied W. Both sides had their spies out and had full information of each other's movements. On the third morning W. gave orders to his whole force to arm and assemble preparatory to attacking; upon hearing which the Pangeran hurriedly sent in word that he would come directly. Preparations of as imposing a character as circumstances permitted were made to receive him. A large empty case, turned up sideways and covered with red cloth, represented the table, inside which a revolver was placed out of sight, but ready to his hand in case of need. Anderson was in charge of a guard of men, armed with rifles, who lined the back of the room, while the head-men, the chiefs, and traders, squatted in a semi-circle on either side of W., and the men, some 200 in number, all fully armed, occupied the back-ground in case the Pangeran should attempt any treacherous move, of which he was fully capable.

The appointed hour arrived, all preparations were completed, but the Pangeran still did not appear, so another peremptory message was despatched, which had the effect of producing him at last. He placed his gold-hilted creese on the table and kneeling at W.'s feet kissed his hand and tendered his submission. After this, negociations proceeded apace, the stolen goods were restored, the Pangeran and his relatives who had participated in the robberies were fined, the river was declared open to trade without duties or exactions of any kind, the birds' nest tribute question was settled, and W. returned in triumph to Sandakan, having greatly increased his authority and power in the whole country, and that without bloodshed.

Chapter III.
Sandakan.

Having so far arranged matters in Sandakan Bay and up the river, W. then
proceeded to give his attention to the country to the North.

In both Sandakan and Labuk Bays there were valuable beds of the seed-
pearl oyster, which had been the source of no inconsiderable revenue in
the past. Some exceedingly heavy rains occurring soon after W.'s arrival,
unfortunately spoilt the crop, as this oyster can only thrive in rather
brackish water, and too great an infusion of either fresh, or salt, water,
has a deleterious effect on them, so that sometimes, season after season,
the crop is lost. The following is an extract from W's. diary explaining the
mode of working the beds before the rains occurred:

On the way across the Bay, just behind the island, found about a
dozen canoes with most of the Sandakan people in them pearl-oyster
fishing. It was an amusing scene, about 150 almost naked brown
bodies plunging and splashing about in all directions, each fresh find
being announced by a series of yells, and, as oysters were common,
there was much noise and excitement. It was a very low tide, with
the water about up to their necks, and the common plan seemed to
be to grope with the feet till an oyster was felt, and then to turn
upside down and bring it up. Moolah and Sandoo (two of our men)
had not been at work more than half an hour and had got nearly 100
each: Moolah took bolder dives than most of them, groping along
the bottom with his hands for nearly 20 yards at a time, always
bringing up one and sometimes two. There was one canoe manned
entirely by women who had their children with them, many of
whom, even of the smallest, were kicking and splashing about
famously in the water. There were nearly 20 people altogether in this
canoe, and the women had got quite a lot of oysters.

The main beds existed at Lingcabo in Labuk Bay and news having reached Sandakan, of troubles up the Labuk, W. combined the two matters and went off there, calling on the way at the island of Lingcabo to see after the seed-pearl collection as well. Lingcabo was a well-known resort of sea rovers, the chief of the place being a Sooloo of some force of character, open to trade with any one quite in the Sooloo style, as the Sooloos, although not actual pirates themselves, have always maintained an attitude of not unfriendly neutrality towards professional pirates, for which amount of countenance they had several advantages, as for instance, the Sultan of Sooloo used always to have the pick of any captives brought by the Balignini; at the same time, if the pirates caught a Sooloo boat at sea, they would capture it and deal with the crew in exactly the same way they would if it had been a Bugis or Brunei one.

After admonishing this chief to have nothing to do with evildoers, W. proceeded on his way up the Labuk to the limit of navigation for his boat, and then, moving into a smaller one, went still further up the river which is a very rapid one abounding in shallows. He enquired at the villages which had been raided by the so-called headhunters and heard their tales and saw some of the wounded, mostly women and children, and then went on to the villages of the people who had committed the raid. No doubt was left in his mind that the latter had been subjected to a good many abuses, their crops taken and themselves oppressed in a good many different ways, of which the custom known as "sarar" seemed to be the principal. On his return to Sandakan, W. sent up an intelligent native with a few men who opened a station between the two districts and prevented oppression on the one hand and retaliatory raids on the other.

For many years past there had existed a tradition with regard to a great lake said to lie to the eastward of Mount Kina Balu, on some of the maps it was marked as being as much as 40 miles across and was supposed to be of great importance, with a large population on its banks. W. travelled within the limits of the lake, as marked on the map, for many miles. Enquiries from natives failed to elicit any information as to the existence of any large sheet of water anywhere in these parts, and W. therefore duly reported home the non-existence of the supposed Kina Balu lake, which fact was made known to the Geographical Society and was subsequently commented upon by the President in his annual address.

About this time danger arose from a most unexpected quarter, which might easily have ended fatally, both as regards W. and the whole enterprise, but by a little tact and judgment, and a firm stand, matters were arranged amicably, although at one time it appeared as though the Sooloo interest had been forced to assume a hostile bearing to the Association.

Great hopes had been placed upon the probable existence of minerals in the country, and W. had been unremitting in his enquiries and researches, but with very little effect beyond some tales which seemed to confirm the old tradition of the existence of gold in the north-west part of Darvel Bay. However, coal in small quantity was brought to him by some of the true inhabitants of the district, the Buludupies, who at length, on the promise of a reward, conducted him to the spot where they had obtained it; there was not much sign of a true seam here, however, although some coal was found lying about.

The Buludupies are a somewhat interesting race, they inhabit the district from the Labuk on the North, some distance up the Kinabatangan, to the Segama on the South. They are the true aborigines of the district and are a mild and pleasant race with full eyes and other slight Caucasian characteristics. They had been a good deal oppressed and bullied by Sooloos and others, and their numbers had been considerably diminished in consequence; at one time they had been a very numerous tribe, but now, comparatively, there were scarcely any left. Their tastes are essentially agricultural and, being timid by nature, they readily yielded to the stronger arm. There was a small but very interesting community of them up the Segaliud river; they were reduced to despair when W. arrived amongst them and had almost abandoned cultivation, as the Sooloos used to come and seize their products, as soon as ripe, on one pretext or another, and in a year or two more no doubt they would have disappeared; but, profiting by the new order of things, they plucked up their courage again and have gone on increasing their fields and plantations year after year, and are now quite a prosperous body of people. They became great cronies of W.'s, acting as his guides in the forest when hunting, instructing him in forest craft and native agriculture, and telling him long legends about the country.

In addition to the events before spoken of, which somewhat tended to detract from W.'s authority, but which need not be further alluded to, Dato Haroun was trying to shake his influence with the Bajaus on the one side, while, on the other, Pangeran Sama was intriguing to increase complications, and altogether matters were then less comfortable than at any other time during the early days. It was at this somewhat critical juncture that an event happened which promised to put an end to all these conflicting parties, as well as British interests also, at one fell swoop, but which in the event turned out to be of the greatest service by welding them all together again and rendering W.'s position more secure than ever.

On the 4th September, the Spanish man-of-war "Marquis del Duero" steamed up the harbour and anchored in front of the town. At first W.

thought it was an ordinary visit, and attached no particular importance to it, though being quite watchful as to anything that might happen; but, in the evening, a report reached him that a special commissioner was on board, whose mission it was to take possession of the place on behalf of the Spanish Government and annex it. W. at once sent for most of the principal people in the Bay, who attended a meeting that night, and all of them promised to stand by him to the last man, the Bajaus, as usual, being foremost in their offers of assistance. An appointment was then made for early next morning for another meeting at Timbong. W. then went on board and asked the Captain (Capt. Lobe) if the report was true, and, as he said it was, W. lodged a protest against any such proceeding, and said that it would be resisted, if necessary, by force; Capt. Lobe, however, said he must stand by his orders.

Early next morning he went to the meeting called over night and a document was drawn up and signed by all present, declaring their contentment with the present government and their determination to resist any effort to oust it, and it was arranged that all the men in the Bay, properly armed, should at once rendezvous at Sandakan.

Capt. Lobe, and Capt. Alejo, the commissioner, came to tiffin with him that day; to protect them he had to draw up round the house a large force of men he could rely upon to prevent any chance of an attack upon them by the excited Sooloos. It may illustrate the extreme scarcity of food to mention that, having nothing whatever else in the house to give them, W. had to sacrifice a pet argus pheasant and have it cooked.

Throughout all these matters Capt. Lobe and W. were privately on the most friendly terms, while officially everything was done with the utmost courtesy.

The "Far East" arrived at daylight on the 6th. Shortly afterwards a message was brought on shore that, if the Spanish flag was not hoisted at noon, the "Marquis del Duero" would open fire upon the town; the consequence of this was an immediate exodus of the women and children, but the men showed the greatest determination. W. ran the British flag up over the houses of two British subjects in the town, and the "Far East," under the orders of Mr. Cowie, obligingly took up a position partly across the line of fire and covering part of the town; and bodies of Sooloomen and Bajaus – dressed in their best clothes, as is customary with them when any fighting is toward – moved about from place to place in the town and amongst the hills immediately at the back of it. The threatened bombardment did not occur, and shortly after 12 my husband went on board and had a long palavar with the Captain, in the course of which he was told that the Spanish flag must be hoisted the next day, to which he replied that he would do nothing of the kind. The interpreter then said that if it was not hoisted the Captain would have to take steps of an unpleasant character with regard to him. W. replied that the Captain could do whatever he liked, but that the Spanish flag would not be hoisted nor the Paou Shun flag be pulled down. At last, after a long discussion, the Captain said he would be off the next morning to report to the Captain-General of the Philippines, and to ask for an increased force to return with, and at 4 a.m. the next morning, to W.'s intense relief, off they steamed accordingly, thus putting an end to a period of considerable tension and strain.

W. next set about looking for an eligible site for a new town at the mouth of the Bay, but had much trouble in finding a place that he thought would do. On the North side of the Bay the hills were too steep and too close to the water's edge, while on the South side the land was too flat and swampy and the water too shallow for a long distance from the shore, while there was no fresh water. Indeed so many objections were there to every place examined, that he rejected them all at this time, but subsequently determined to make the best of it and start at a place just inside the harbour on the North side.

Dato Haroun al Raschid, the former Sooloo viceroy of Sandakan, followed closely all that occurred in Sandakan and sent messengers to endeavour to order, or persuade, the Bajaus to go down to Tawi-Tawi, there to meet him, his real object being to get the main body of W.'s allies away from him so that he could not oppose any direct movement of the Dato's on Sandakan, when he chose to attempt a coup d'etat. The Bajau Emaum informed W. of this and of his (the Emaum's) intention not to leave him (W.).

So far the pirates had not been particularly troublesome, a few boats were captured from time to time, and various murders were recorded, but they had been held somewhat in check by the knowledge of the advent of white men on the coast: however, finding after a time that W. was absolutely alone, they plucked up courage and grew bolder in their operations, capturing boats, even in the Bay of Sandakan itself.

To illustrate the ease with which the most terrible wounds heal amongst these rice-eating temperate people, it may be mentioned that on one occasion after one of the numerous skirmishes with them, one of W.'s men was brought in with a wound reaching from the shoulder to the thigh, in the whole length of which the hand and arm might have been laid; with care and attention, however, this man quite recovered and was all right again in a few weeks.

Intelligence as to the doings of the pirates grew more and more serious, and the Bay of Sandakan was absolutely blockaded; an attack on the town itself was feared nightly. The entire tribe of Bajaus had gone away rattan collecting, Hadji Dato's men from Timbong were all up the Kinabatangan and, on W's going round to consolidate his forces, he found that there were only 11 able-bodied men left in the whole Bay, in addition to the few Buludupies up the Segaliud river, and they refused to come down to help. With these few men, including three or four Chinese, W. had to keep unremitting guard night and day, with weapons all ready, in expectation of an hourly attack. Luckily, at this particular juncture, the first commencement of a constabulary force to help him arrived from Singapore in the shape of half a dozen Somalis, and from this time forward he felt far more secure.

These sea fights more usually resemble a game than a stern encounter; when an action occurred between two fleets of about equal number, they would range themselves in opposed lines about 300 yards apart with much beating of gongs and shouting, until one boat, having some one desirous of distinguishing himself on board, would paddle towards the other line, the hero standing up in the bow, gun in hand, shouting out "I am Allee of Loke, I defy you all, I killed your fathers and brothers and am going to kill you all, and burn your village and carry off all your young women. You set of boys come here and be slain by a man," – and so on, only that Malay languages are much too courteous to lend themselves to very keen vituperation – naughty "swear" words being unknown. All the time he held forth he would be dominating the position, looking out for an easy shot, while the people in the other line ducked behind their wood barriers; finally, thinking he was near enough, he would blaze away; once his gun was empty the others would jump up and paddle after him as fast as they could, his boat fleeing for protection to his own line, part of the game being to see, if, in the ardour of the chase, he could entice one or two of the other boats so far, that, before they could turn and regain their own line, they would be surrounded, in which case it would go hard with their crews. As for the firing, what between the badness of the guns and the uncertainty of aim caused by the tippling about of the canoes, it was very rarely the case that anyone got hurt, but if two boats closed, half the men were down, in a very few seconds, with ghastly wounds caused by the Sooloo heavy chopping barongs or long Illanun creeses.

In the spring W. heard reports that an alliance had been made between the Illanuns and the Balignini. Most or perhaps even all seagoers of Malay race have a weakness for piracy if a favourable opportunity offers, but these two tribes are the only ones that took up piracy as a regular profession, and of these two it was the Illanuns that carried on their operations in the boldest manner.[12] In former times for a range of 1,000 miles in any direction they used to boldly sail the seas, all other tribes fleeing for refuge whenever the presence of an Illanun fleet in their waters was known, and on one or two occasions they even fought stiff actions with British men-of-war. The Balignini, on the other hand, used to skulk along the shore cutting off fishermen's boats, kidnapping girls on the beach, and so on, and carrying off their captives for sale in Sooloo and elsewhere, and taking great care to keep out of danger. The Illanuns murdered nearly everyone that fell into their hands and did their pirating almost solely for the plunder, while the main object of the Balignini was to catch people to sell as slaves, and to this day there are many people from the Philippines, Java, Singapore and elsewhere, in Sooloo, who were caught when they were young and sold there by the Balignini. Pressure had been gradually brought to bear upon both Illanuns and Balignini, however, and as, in addition to the loss they suffered in their numerous encounters with men-of-war of all nationalities, they were constantly having fights amongst themselves, they rapidly dwindled away in numbers and in these latter days had not a shadow of their former strength; still, when W. heard of their joining forces, he was rendered rather anxious, his anxiety not being lessened when he heard that a fleet of the combined forces of the two had been into Lingcabo for provisions, and sure enough shortly afterwards accounts came in, thick and fast, of a pirate raid on a large scale on the coast. What was to be done was not very clear. W. fitted out a boat and thought of going along the coast himself, but the Chinese and Malay traders waited upon him and dissuaded him as his going away with his six Somalis would have too much enfeebled the place and laid it open to attack, and the value of the cargo in the shops had much increased, so there seemed nothing to do but to sit down and wait. However, the pirates were not to have it entirely their own way. On the 19th May, three boats, travelling together for safety, coming into the harbour were attacked by five pirates, there were only about 12 Sandakan men against some 50 pirates and one boat was captured with three men in it, two other being wounded, but the other two boats escaped – the pirates did not escape altogether scot free, two or three of them getting large slashes. Their fleet was under the command of a man named Armee, who also acted as pilot, he being a man that W. had helped only a few months before when he himself had been attacked and some half dozen of his men killed.

At this juncture the little "Far East" turned up, and W. arranged with Mr. Cowie to look in along the coast wherever he could, a warrant being given to two of the police to examine and, if necessary, apprehend any suspicious looking people.

As particular luck had it, when the "Far East" neared the mouth of the harbour, two boats were seen, one of which was immediately identified by two of the Sooloos who had been at the fight, as their boat which had been captured. Off they went, and away went the "Far East" in chase. They were full of men and paddled hard, and one of them got round the end of Bahalla and escaped, but the other one, keeping too close in shore, got inside a reef and found itself in a cul de sac. Mr. Cowie immediately lowered a boat and, taking command himself, with the two policemen, the two Sooloos, and some of his crew, cut her out from the beach under fire from the pirates concealed in the bushes. Two of the pirates were killed in this encounter. The "Far East" returned that night with the recaptured boat in tow, and the next morning, with a strong force, with W. in command, went back; the force landed and drove the island from end to end, but the pirates had escaped in the night. They found one of the boat's crew, however, who had managed to give his captors the slip in the scrub, who gave full particulars of the pirates, who were under the chief command of Emaum Janjowi of Tawi Tawi and of Dato Kurunding of Tuncu. A barong that was in the captured boat W. presented to Mr. Cowie on the spot of the previous day's encounter. Sixty five Bajau women and children were captured on this raid, the adult males all being killed, creese in hand, defending their families. The captives were taken down to Buloongan and there sold.

On the 15th June, the greater portion of the town was burnt down by accident, most of the houses being destroyed. The fire originated owing to the carelessness of a man named Sabtu, who disappeared when he saw what mischief he had occasioned, fearing that he would be murdered by the Sooloos. The scene was naturally one of great confusion, there was no time to save anything, the fire running from house to house with the upmost rapidity, and in three-quarters of an hour from its commencement it was all over, and the police were groping about in the shallow water for their rifles, &c., which they had pitched hastily out of their houses to prevent their being burned. One man had to dash a hole through the side of his house and drop his children into the water through it to avoid the flames. Many thousands of dollars worth of trade goods and produce were destroyed and nearly all the stores of rice.

W. immediately made up his mind that it was no use rebuilding at Sandakan, and the remove had better be at once made to the new Elopura site. Next morning, W., wondering what had become of Sabtu was asking after him, when from underneath a table, which was covered with a cloth whose ends hung down to the floor, a small voice was heard stating that Sabtu was there; and not only he, but his wife also, emerged from their hiding place in my husband's bedroom.

Two or three boats were at once prepared and a start was made for the entrance to the Bay. On the 21st of June, 1879, W. cut down the first tree on the site of the new town.

Plate 5 'Elopura (Sandakan)', unattributed engraving, 1883.
Source: Sabah Museum, Sabah, Malaysia.

Chapter IV.
Elopura.

The spot selected for the new town was situated at the mouth of the Bay, about twelve miles distant from the old Sandakan site. The whole district was primeval forest down to the water's edge, the nearest houses of any kind were those at the old town. It was therefore starting a town in an absolutely fresh and uninhabited country.

W.'s first proceeding was to fell the trees at some little distance inland, clear the ground of the fallen trunks and branches, and build some temporary houses there, intentionally leaving a thick fringe of forest at the water's edge to act as a screen, so that passing pirate boats, of which there were many, should not see that anything unusual was in progress. He then stockaded in a rocky headland and mounted on its summit three guns in a sort of fort, one of these guns a 7 pr. breech-loader kindly lent by Mr. Cowie.

These preparations having been completed, the forest fringe was then knocked over, the fort unmasked, and the commencement of the town disclosed.

Instead of waiting to be attacked by the pirates, W. now assumed an offensive attitude towards them; all passing sails were pursued and the pirates soon realized that they were over-matched in those waters for the time being, but they breathed vows of vengeance and declared their intention of returning with an overwhelming force in a short time.

Difficulties now occurred fast and thick. Pangeran Sama, hearing that W. had been burnt out, came down from the Kinabatangan with a large force, hoping that an opportunity would present itself of finally ridding himself of the new comers. The Spaniards proposed to deal finally with the issues raised by the "Marquis del Duero's" visit and make good their claim to the country, ousting the British, while Dato Haroun Al Raschid, who was in their councils, thought the time had come for him to push forward his claim to the Viceroyalty. The consequence was that the Spanish man-of-war "Sirena" left Sooloo, with the Dato on board, bound for Sandakan, her intention being to bombard the place if she could not get possession of it otherwise.

A protest, however, against Spanish interference in North Borneo having been lodged by the British Government at Madrid, was from thence forwarded on to Manila, and the authorities there, seeing that an awkward crisis would arise if the "Sirena" carried out her programme, sent a boat down specially to cut her off at Balabac where she had to call before proceeding to Sandakan. Thus the struggling enterprise was delivered of the gravest peril that perhaps ever threatened it. The Dato, however, was plucky and stuck to his intentions, and as the "Sirena" would not proceed, he left her, coming on with his retinue and followers in five prahus, which duly arrived in Sandakan. Somewhat to W.'s consolation the position of affairs was then very involved, neither the Dato nor the Pangeran dared take any hostile step for fear of finding the other on W.'s side, while all were afraid that any weakening of their forces might lend opportunity to the pirates to destroy them all. Under these circumstances the Dato thought it best to sit down and wait and see what might turn up and what allies he could gain: altogether a quadrangular struggle.

The three factions in the town met together freely and the leaders exchanged visits. W. of course was on the alert to guard against any sudden rush on his stockade and so matters went on for awhile; W. being pretty well informed by his friends of all the Pangeran's and Dato's movements from day to day.

At one of the public receptions the Dato asked W. what he would do should he one day find his flag down and his (the Dato's) flying in its place. To this W. replied that he should go straight for the Dato, wherever he might happen to be, and blow the top of his head off with his revolver. This made the Dato pause in his projected operations until he should have the position more in his own hands, and his efforts to enter into an alliance with the Pangeran were redoubled. W. at this time was informed that the alliance was on the point of being cemented, when, at the critical moment, a personal quarrel broke out between the two on the question of some old debts, and as the Bajau Imaum turned up at this juncture, and Dato Hadji also arrived on the scene with a number of followers from Melapi (both of them having been sent for by W.), the position was greatly improved from W.'s point of view.

There were at this time several hundred men at Elopura, and the small number of houses were overflowing.

A total change in the aspect of affairs was wrought by the arrival on the scene of H.M.S. "Kestrel," Capt. Edwardes. Pangeran Sama forthwith returned to Melapi, and Dato Haroun, quite realizing that the game was up, hoisted up sail and went off to Palawan of which island he assumed the government, and remained in charge for the following year or two. He now, with the aid of his friends the Spaniards, occupies the throne of Sooloo.

Capt. Edwardes then proceeded to enquire into the Balignini and Illunan raids. After careful investigation, to assure himself that it was really piracy, viz., indiscriminate robbery of boats captured on the high seas; such action being in no way influenced by tribal feuds, feelings, or jealousies, he was dealing with,* Captain Edwardes steamed down to Tuncu, their head-quarters, and attacked and captured the place, destroying sixteen pirate boats with fortified sides all ready to proceed to sea.

Thinking this a good opportunity to extend his influence southwards, W. made a trip into Darvel Bay with a number of his men, and landing at Silam hoisted the Association's flag there and obtained the allegiance of the people.

Reinforcements of police were sent shortly after this from Singapore, from which time forward the security of Elopura was never again in doubt, and the very trying and anxious time W. had for three years, during the while of which period he was always more or less threatened with attack from one quarter or another, came to an end.

The town grew apace and an era of rapid prosperity set in, a grateful change after the long period of anxiety that had preceded it; jungle produce flowed down the opened rivers Kinabatangan, Labuk, and Sugut, and came across the sea to Sandakan, the people being no longer afraid of capture by pirates on the way. Capt. Johnston, of H.M.S. "Egeria," who then visited Elopura, reported that he found a rising town of some 600 persons with a good many shops and an increasing trade.

In addition to the foregoing incidents, there were from day to day difficulties and awkwardnesses of all kinds continually cropping up, in several of which blood flowed freely, many of them demanding the exercise of force in being dealt with, but those narrated are the principal ones, and those more particularly having a bearing upon the progress of the country. The slightest miscalculation or mistake, in the total absence of any support to fall back upon, or the presence of any one to fill W.'s place had he been killed or disabled, would inevitably have resulted in the

---

*   With regard to these Balignini and Illanun, no such question could arise as was the case when Rajah Brooke dealt with the Seribas and Sekarran Dyaks.

loss of the territory. In the moments of peril which occurred almost daily, had he held back or flinched, his authority would have been upset, with the same result.

Some short time after this, W., wishing to see for himself the state of affairs on the Kinabatangan river, made an expedition up it. He went in a steam-launch as far as it was navigable, some 130 miles, for the whole of which distance the river is deep and sluggish, the shores flat and forest-covered, and the waters virtually tidal. So far it was very uninteresting, being almost uninhabited, as there were only two villages for the whole of this distance. The swampy nature of the country causes it to be very unhealthy. Arrived at the limit of launch navigation, the river got swifter and shallow rapids at each bend necessitated the use of light draft canoes, but the banks became higher and the country healthier. Here another element of disturbance came in, for down the Quarmote, a large tributary river, marauding gangs of head-hunters used to come, killing everybody in the neighbourhood; so it was not until many miles past the point where this river joined the main stream that population commenced, but from here onwards there was a fair sprinkling of people. One of W.'s intentions was to make personal enquiries on the spot as to how Pangeran Samah stood with the people of the upper river, and whether he had any real influence on them, about which he heard conflicting accounts. The Pangeran was a man of peculiar character, who would very likely have made his mark had he been born in any other country, or been given larger opportunities. As it was, he, by the exercise of several different qualities, had obtained the chieftainship of a tribe of somewhat timid people, in whose possession there happened to be the valuable Gomanton caves, producing some $25,000 worth of nests yearly. This tempting bait brought down a continual stream of high-class marauders to try and get a portion of this prize, and in the endeavour to baffle them, the Pangeran found a rich field for the exercise of his particular gifts of cunning, cruelty, and ferocity, combined with great organizing powers. Owing to the difficulty of collecting the nests at the top of caves, some two or three hundred feet high, with wet and slippery sides, it is only the most practised climbers that can get them, so that new comers could not secure any for themselves, but had to allow the Buludupies to collect the nests first, and then to transfer as many of them as they could to their own pockets afterwards. At one time, the Pangeran told W., there were ten powerful chiefs with numerous followers at Melapi, each trying to get as much as he could for himself, but some fell sick and died, others quarrelled, fought, and killed each other, others were deserted by their followers and left stranded and lost their influence, and ultimately all came to grief in some way or another, the result, as W. afterwards heard, of either direct violence or intrigue by the Pangeran himself. Evidently he classed W. as one of the same set, to be poisoned, murdered, or outmanoeuvred in a similar way.

W. went on his way up the river much interested in all he saw; the soil was extremely fertile, the crops heavy, the people lazy, and the air was pure and healthy the higher the river was ascended, and the nights cool and pleasant. Everyone went about armed, the slightest dispute led to bloodshed, human sacrifice was still a custom, tribe fought against tribe, and everywhere there was a fear of head-hunting raids; at one house he stopped at, he found two freshly cut off human heads hanging up, taken from a neighbouring village. But on the whole he was very much impressed by the possibilities latent in the country inland for supporting a very large population. Well acquainted with some of the thickly inhabited parts of China, he was of opinion that this district was as well qualified in every respect to support as large a population as the finest parts of the Chekiang or Fokien provinces.[13]

W. soon found that the Pangeran possessed but very little influence on the upper river, and that the people, a simple and unpolished set of countrymen, wished to have nothing to do with him, as in order to assert and maintain a show of authority and to strike terror amongst them, he, on several occasions, seized one of their men on some frivolous pretext and had him hacked to pieces in public.

While visiting different villages, gaining the confidence, finding out the ideas of the people, and making arrangements for the future, rumours reached W. that the Pangeran was endeavouring to raise the country behind him and thereby cut off his retreat. He left immediately, hurrying down stream without stopping, and, travelling night and day reached Melapi early one morning, where he found that the Pangeran had called an assemblage of the head-men of the tribe for that afternoon. He at once took steps to frustrate the Pangeran's movement, and calling to his aid all the Sooloos and traders and their men then in the neighbourhood, placed a cordon round the Pangeran's house and entering it with four men found him asleep.

On advancing towards him, the Pangeran sprang up, drew his long creese, which he always kept at hand, and would have cut W. down had he not instantly covered him with his revolver. Two of W.'s men jumped on to the large elevated bed-place waiting W.'s order to attack the Pangeran, one of whose wives, springing to his side, threw off her clothes to her waist in a moment, and, seizing a spear from the roof, stood ready at his right hand. W. then ordered two of his men with loaded rifles to aim at the Pangeran, and asked him why, standing there with weapons drawn against the Government, he should not be shot down. The Pangeran replied that W. might shoot him if he liked, but that no Sooloo was going to put his hands upon him without a fight. W. then accused him of intending to murder him on his way down the river, whereupon the Pangeran, evidently thinking his last moment had arrived, sang a death song to the effect that he had always held sway on the Kinabatangan and that no one, orang putih or orang Suluk (white man or Sooloo), should ever oust him from it, and a good deal more to the same effect. W. kept the Pangeran on his legs until he was fairly worn out and asked to be allowed to sit down and drink some water. Finally he made emphatic promises of improved behaviour. Two or three of his men who came in to his rescue gave up their arms; W. threatening to shoot them if they refused.

W. then went off to the place the Pangeran's chiefs were to assemble at, and reached it just as they were arriving. After conferring with them they declared that they would never again support the Pangeran in any project he might entertain against the Government.

During his stay at Melapi on this occasion, W. received fairly reliable information from the Pangeran's Chinese goldsmith of the existence of gold in that district, and having had sent to his assistance about that time a European, from Singapore, who was supposed to have some knowledge of metals, W. sent him to Melapi on a mission to the Pangeran, but with secret orders to find out the Chinaman, without the Pangeran's knowledge, and get all the information he could from him. This was not the first occasion W. had delegated men, the only assistants he had had up to this time, to Melapi on different missions; but the Pangeran, a shrewd observer of human nature, had found out their weak points, and through them discovered what their errands were, one of them yielding to wine and a second to beauty, but W. had hoped he might have relied on a European. The Pangeran, crafty old diplomat, very soon managed to find out his weak spot also and soon afterwards arrived at the knowledge of his true errand. He at once assured the European that the Chinaman should be sent for, but instead of doing anything of the kind, had the man, who was in the very next house at the moment, sent away to the next village and poisoned that night.

As a consequence of this trip, stations were made at Quarmote, and subsequently at Penungah on the Kinabatangan, while as a result of his Labuk journey, a start had already been made at the mouth of the Angsoan on the Labuk, leading to further increase of the trade of the town, boats beginning to find their way thence to Elopura. Admiral Coote in the "Vigilant," after calling at Sandakan, went to Manila and gave notice there that no interference by the Spaniards would be allowed in North Borneo; the police force was increased to 40 men and finally the B.N.B.C. was started in May, 1882, the Royal Charter having already been given on the 1st November, 1881.

Chapter V.
Birdsnesting, and a Hunt in Borneo.

A Bornean house-boat.—Beautiful scenery.—Lazy Erahans.—Pig hunting.—Rhinoceros sumatranus in Borneo.—A native reception.—A terrible weapon.—Gay dresses.—Visit to Segalung birds'-nest caves.—Native boats.—Pangeran Laut.—Giant orchid.—Native wax candles.—Limestone caves.—A rough scramble.—Timba mata.—A beautiful island.—Native yarns.— Oysters.—Fishing.—Visit to Madai birds' nest caves.—Keema.— Sea produce.—Elephants.—Dangerous rock-climbing.

On board a trim little craft, not a trading boat evidently, for the forepart of her is chiefly devoted to a large saloon with omnibus windows like a Shanghai houseboat, and conveniently furnished with everything that could reasonably be desired: not a yacht either, for everywhere within easy reach there are stands of rifles, boarding pikes, &c., while on the fore-deck there is a seven-pounder properly fitted on its traverse and evidently meant for business. The crew too, in their smart uniforms, are more numerous than either a yacht or a trading boat would require.

Nor are we in England; nowhere in England is there such lovely scenery as one glance round from the deck discovers. We appear to be in a huge lake studded everywhere with beautiful islands, green to the water's edge except for the gleaming white strip of beach that marks the margin of the deep blue water. On the mainland close by is a fine mountain clothed to its summit with high forest trees and with a pretty little village nestling at its feet, off which we lie anchored. All around us are ranges of hills and mountains, rising one beyond the other as far as the eye can reach. The air is warm and balmy although the month is January; and the sturdy active crew are Malays.

We are on board the B.N.B. Coy.'s revenue boat "Sabine," in Looc Sabahan (Darvel Bay) on a bird's-nesting expedition.

W. went ashore and had a talk with Dato Tumongong Gumbah in charge of the Company's station at Silarn, also with Inchi Hassan, the agent for the bird's-nest cave contractor for this year. They were both of opinion that, without a good deal of urging the Erahans, from sheer laziness, would delay the collection of nests until they had all gone bad. W. sent for Pangeran Amas one of their head chiefs who had "tangoonged" (guaranteed) this year's collection, and put through much other business and in the afternoon he went out hunting.

I here quote from his diary the account of the afternoon's sport:

The leading spirit of the hunt was decidedly a Bisayah or Indian from the Philippines (better known to English readers as Manila-men, though perhaps they have never been near Manila in their lives) named Esnine – a particularly muscular specimen of humanity, who entered keenly into the sport. The dogs were four queer little brown animals rather long in the body, rather short in the leg, with sharp jackally noses, prick ears, and a half sly, half humorous, twinkle in the back of their eyes. They were the property of Sheriff Byassin, who armed with a spear, came with us. We went to look for a buffalo which Esnine had put up that morning, which he thought he had marked down, but it was very soon evident that, with the dogs and the motley following of Sooloos, Malays, &c., not forgetting Esnine, we must make the best of whatever turned up.

The forest was very open and easy going, and we had not been a quarter of an hour in it when suddenly one of the little dogs gave tongue, and with a short sharp little "week, week, week," away the whole pack went, and away after them went we. However, in less than five minutes some of the notes became more long drawn, while others were quicker and more yapping in their tone, and it was clear the quarry was being bayed. On rushing up we found a little pig had taken refuge amongst the roots of a tree with the dogs surrounding it, one of them occasionally rushing in and having a snap at it. Poor little piggie was quickly secured alive, its legs tied up, and it was left under a tree till we returned again. On once more, and up a steep hill, on the top of which it was just possible the buffalo might be, but before we got there "week, week, week, week," again from the dogs. In the forest there is no seeing more than thirty yards in any direction owing to the tree trunks, saplings, dwarf palms, wild ginger, &c., so we could not tell what we were after; but following the dogs again to the bottom of the valley and then down stream, torn by thorns, dashing wildly through the bushes, stumbling in our haste over the big rough stones of the brook, sometimes in the water, sometimes out, and sometimes again making short cuts through the forest, the little dogs "weeking" away in front and bringing the game up every now and then for a few moments. Esnine was far ahead; at last there was a shot, and on getting up we found that a large pig had been bagged. The little dogs had been unable to hold the pig at bay, but as it broke away, Esnine wounded it with his spear, whereupon it wheeled round and charged. He dodged it and again sent his spear well in, but before it could charge again one of the fortmen came up and sent a Snider ball through its body; even then it was some time before it succumbed. The above will serve for a description of all the runs we had, of which there were five in all, a kill resulting every time. Esnine got first spear three times.

The next afternoon, after sundry preparations in connection with the nest-collecting had been made and other matters settled, we went away to explore a path said to lead towards the gold district, the more particularly that on it there was said to be good large game country. The track was a very fair one, and good going; and after an hour and a half's walk, during which we had seen the old tracks of elephants in two places, besides those of buffalo, deer, and heaps of pig, we came to what was said to be the best place; but after an hour's wandering about, not seeing any more traces, half of us gave it up and returned. The others did not come back till nightfall, having come to a place where there were fresh rhinoceros tracks, but they saw nothing of the animal.

I may take this opportunity of mentioning, as it has lately been said in the pages of *The Field* that there was still some uncertainty as to what species the Bornean rhinoceros belongs to, that of something like a dozen skulls examined all were R. sumatranus. Our elephant also is probably the Sumatran variety of E. indicus, but this is not quite certain.

We had a reception afterwards; amongst other people, Dato Buginda Etam brought his four wives aboard. Dato Buginda Etam is the good Dato as distinguished from Dato Buginda Putih the bad Dato; they both come from Tuncu, a celebrated pirate village. The old pirate chief, Dato Kurunding, is dead; this is the man who used to show people a crees-barong (a weapon somewhere between a large bowie-knife and a Roman sword), with which he boasted he had himself killed one hundred and twenty people. Buginda Putih, his son, exhibited a desire to emulate his father's exploits; but was soon controlled by the growing strength of the government, and had to fly, deserted by most of his followers, to Spanish territory. His cousin, Dato Buginda Etam it is who was on board with us to-day with his wives, as well as Sheriff Byassin's, &c. As usual, they were gorgeously arrayed in all the brilliant hues of the rainbow, purple and orange-coloured jackets, sarongs of dark green, or else red and yellow plaids, worked with silk. Their masses of jet black hair, well anointed with fresh cocoanut oil, was combed up high on the crowns of their heads, and tied in knots, which as they do not know the use of hairpins, continually descends, and has to be re-dressed. They usually cut a small square fringe round their foreheads. They had nothing whatever to say for themselves, but sat huddled up all together with their attendant slaves, staring at us, and could hardly be prevailed upon to sip the over-sweetened tea we gave them. Dato Buginda himself wore short purple tights, embroidered with gold, coming half-way down his thighs, and a little thin muslin jacket over a vest, the jacket decorated with tiny frills, coloured braid, and buttons of gold. On his head he wore a dark purple silk handkerchief, also elaborately embroidered in gold, and with a knowing little tail sticking up over the left ear.

All matters being ready for the real business of the expedition, we started the next morning for Sama Dongguan and Sama Cooed. At the former place we found Pangeran Laut true to his word, expecting us; and as soon as Ramee began to beat the gong, announcing our approach, off he came in his boat, flying the Sabah flag from the stern. These native boats are very quaint and curious, and have a charming effect when scudding out to sea, their parti-coloured sails full of wind. Their foundation is nothing else than a canoe, upon the centre part of which is fixed a sort of large platform, with long outriggers attached, so that there is not the least fear of being upset; a mast is then fixed, and a sail of many colours, usually in broad stripes, prepared. As protection against the sun, they place a kadjang over the centre portion of the boat, beneath which you have to squat. These boats are called dapongs, and it was usually in them that the pirates used to make their raids.

At Sama Cooed we found Pangeran Amas and his men, who are the most important persons of all, for they are the birdsnest collectors. W. had been afraid they would beg for a further delay, for these people are dreadful dawdlers, and always put off doing anything as long as ever they can; but to our satisfaction, we found five or six boats full of men and women ready to accompany us, the Pangeran promising that the rest of his men should join us in a day or two at Segalung. The boats were then attached in a long tail to the stern of the "Sabine," and away we went, bound for the opposite side of the bay, which was so far distant that the hills were all lost in a vague mist. It took us all day to reach the beautiful inland sea behind the island of Tanna Balu, for we had to go at half-speed, both on account of the numberless coral shoals, and also that we might not swamp the boats forming our comet-like tail; so that it was nightfall (the sun always setting in this part of the world about 6 p.m. or 6.10) before we reached an anchorage. Pangeran Laut undertook to pilot us, and exhibited much care and caution. He brought with him his little child, a girl about five or six years old, of whom he appeared extremely fond, although she was a most unattractive object, being covered with a mass of sores, owing to the low diet and bad food these people have. She wore no clothes except a little sarong; and as a rule, in this warm climate it is very difficult to get children to keep any clothes on.

Next morning everyone was astir at daybreak, making preparations for work. We dressed and had breakfast, and then went off in Pangeran Laut's boat, bound for the caves of Segalung. The way was up a narrow river, thickly bordered by mangrove trees, which grew luxuriantly in the rich black mud, as they like brackish water. We saw a magnificent specimen of the orchid grammatophyllum, which was too huge to move. It had been in bloom, and Osman climbed up and got me some of the great seedpods, which are as big as small cucumbers. At last we pulled through knee-deep mud, it being low tide, to the base of a giant limestone hill, which was thickly clothed with trees. Two of the experienced nest collectors had already set to work, had made a fire, and were preparing beeswax candles and wooden-pronged forks, the one to hold the light, the other to detach the nests from the rocks. The candles they made by taking a long-piece of thick wick of rolled cloth, and, having warmed a lump of beeswax, squeezed it thickly round the wick; ordinary candles do not answer, as they spoil the nests. The pronged forks are made out of thin saplings; they are cut in different lengths, the top end is split into four, and to keep the ends apart little wedges of wood are inserted at the base of the slits and bound into place by rattans, and the beeswax candle is secured just below.

Having watched these preparations, we followed three guides, who led the way through the thin forest in an upward direction. Soon we came to a grotto formed by a great mass of overhanging limestone rock, all bare and jagged, on the outside of which the common begonia was growing luxuriantly, and below was a great cool pool of water. At the back were dark caverns and recesses that we could not see the end of. We imagined this was the entrance, but our guides said no; so on we went, following them through the forest round the base of the cliff, coming every now and then upon detached masses of limestone, all worn and riddled like honeycomb. At last we arrived at a great cavern, whose approach was blocked by great boulders of rock; this they said, was the entrance to one cave. Lying about were remains of wooden coffins, with rough carvings upon them, and probably very old, as they are made of billian, which is a very lasting wood, they were in a very worm-eaten and rotting condition. Notwithstanding this there were no remains of bones.

Now our difficulties began, scrambling from boulder to boulder across little precipices, up jagged rocks, and into all sorts of huge chambers and tunnels in the hill. Now and then there was a rent in the side which admitted sufficient light to show us our way, and then would occur a great opening showing us the sky above. Still the guides led us on into narrower twilight passages. At one point it was necessary to climb over Osman's body to reach a point above; at another we had to wriggle our bodies along a narrow ledge with a great hole below, and the ceiling of limestone not 18 inches above, so that you had to lie prone on your stomach and to creep down a black hole in the floor of one cave, which dropped into a passage leading to a cave below, and at last we stood in a birds' nest cave. It was only a small one, but they had specially selected it for its accessibility. Then the guides lit their candles, and showed us how to lift them high so as to throw a full light on the roof. It was full of niches, but, to our disappointment, we could find no nests worth taking, as evidently some men had been before us and robbed the cave. There were, however, plenty of tiny nests in course of construction, very white ones of the best quality, worth $15 a catty, so we retraced our steps. Hassan and Pangeran Amas had better luck, as they brought some very fine nests to the launch in the evening, and were quite hopeful, as some more collectors had arrived, and others were expected.

On the next day the collectors, some seventy or eighty in number, being busy exploring the caves to see where the nest really was, and making other arrangements, we went off to Timbamata, at the further end of Tanna Balu, at the end of which there is a fine grassy slope much frequented by herds of deer. Pangeran Laut took us in his depong, and we sailed away gaily before the strong fresh wind, rushing over the bright water in a most exhilarating and delightful manner. We were in an inland sea, all around us were great and small islands, as well as the headlands, points, and coves of Tanna Balu on the one side, and the mainland on the other, on which hand there were hills beyond hills and mountains beyond mountains, and all islands, headlands and mountains forest-clothed to the water's edge. The nearest approach to it, perhaps, is the Inland Sea in Japan. Yet, as far as the eye could see, this beautiful world is utterly uninhabited – a great unpeopled land, ourselves and our company the only human beings in it. It seems strange that such a land of promise, so full of natural beauties and valuable products of all kinds, should be unknown and unvisited by man. On arriving at Grassy Point, it was found that the deer had sought the shade, as it was the middle of the day, and though several were seen, they were all too far off. From the top of one of the hills there was a magnificent view of the great bay, with its many islands dotted about, with snug harbours and coves, and the beautiful light green of the water, where the coral shoals contrasted with the darker green of the trees, and the deep blue of the sky and the sea. To gaze to the right and to the left, over all those miles of sea and land, and think there was not a living soul near us, was awe-inspiring; but it was a grand and wonderful sight, and one never to be forgotten.

We sailed back to the launch before the sea breeze, the wind having, as we had calculated, obligingly turned round in our favour again, and on the way the Pangeran related little tales of adventures by sea and land, invariably ending with some of the other side being killed – notably an anecdote of how he managed to corner a whole lot of head-hunting Sagais, and with his own hand slaughtered fourteen of them before they could break away; for the Pangeran, though a very mild and pleasant man to look at, and by no means muscular has the character of being one of the most determined fighters of all the desperate characters in the Bay.

We landed at one place, and found the shore strewn with rock oysters, of which there was simply an inexhaustible supply to be had for the picking up. On the far side of Timbamata there are quantities of seed-pearl oysters, for the sea in these parts is full of produce, which is to be had for the mere trouble of collecting.

Having arrived at the launch, we bathed, dressed and dined and afterwards went out fishing by moonlight with a "rumbut," or cast net, catching quantities of rather small fish and some enormous prawns, which we forthwith cooked and indulged in an impromptu supper. After this again Osman went out fishing with line and hook from a canoe, and caught thirteen small sharks!

The first real collecting took place to-night. It is so pitch dark within the large caves, where the bulk of the nests are, that night and day are alike there, and the men prefer to collect at night, as it is cooler. We did not stop to see the result, however, but started off at daybreak for Madai. Afterwards we learnt that in the course of the first day or two's collection, about a picul of white nests, or – say, twelve hundred dollars' worth – had been obtained.

Our way to Madai lay between more islands and about midday we arrived off the mouth of the river; but it was too shallow for us to go in, so we had to anchor outside, and, ever calm though the bay is, there was quite swell enough to make the "Sabine" wobble about disagreeably. At low tide all hands – about one hundred people – landed on a coral reef to search for their evening meal, and lots of keema, trepang, and other things were soon found. Keema is a huge mollusc, a bivalve, something like an enormous cockle. On the coast of Tawi Tawi there is said to be one as big as a house! but no mention is made of what sized house. The largest shells we got to-day, however, were not above a foot broad though we have found some three feet. The trepang was obtained by looking for little depressions in the sand, and making a rapid plunge with the fingers at the centre of it, when something hard and slippery is felt and seized. The other hand then loosens the sand in the neighbourhood, following the slimy body along till it has no further power of grasping, and then, with a jerk, a hideous, whitish, slithery object, like an enormous fat worm, is pulled out. This, the Sooloos say, is the best kind of trepang, much better than the common kind, which is found on the bottom of the sea and not in the sand. We also got many beautiful shells, some with long spines, others round and tortoise-shell-coloured, cowries, and the like. After this we rowed up the river to the landing-stage, where there were sixteen depongs, each with not less than ten people in it. Preparations for collecting were in progress, rattan ladders made in long lengths, beeswax candles twisted, &c.

Shortly after daybreak next morning nearly one hundred men started, carrying provisions, rattans, &c. The caves are about four miles inland, and the path lies through the forest, which was thickly covered with fresh elephant tracks, and in one place an elephant was heard, but went off before the party with rifles could get up; it had been wallowing in the mud of a small marsh. Later on, however, one gang of men on the path were charged by a tusker, which ran amongst them, scattering them right and left, so that they threw down their loads and climbed up the trees.

There is no difficulty in going into the Madai caves, which are much larger than those we saw at Segalung; huge caverns opening, one beyond the other, into enormous, domed transepts or chambers, dimly lighted here and there by splits or rents in their sides. The nest is faintly seen in the lighter places like a dark shade on the roof, which is most irregular, some lines with deep incisions going sharply out of sight into black darkness, and in others rough rocks full of niches and holes, so that how anybody can reach them seems incredible. It is managed, however, by men swinging strings weighted with stones to other men 20 ft. or 30 ft. off, both clinging on to the slippery rock, at perhaps, 100 ft. from the ground, and then dragging rattan ladders up and fixing them across from one to the other, so that they can crawl on the ladders to the more inaccessible places. The men must be finished athletes.

Leaving nearly a hundred men at the caves, where they will reside for another month, W. walked back through the forest, and got on board shortly before dinner, and the next day we steamed back to Silam, when it was arranged that a third party of collectors should start for Baturong, so that by the time our labours were finished some three hundred men were busy collecting. This was the first time the nest had ever been properly collected from all these caves, as it is impossible for the natives to organize matters sufficiently well themselves, and a large quantity of it has always gone bad, to the heavy loss of the natives themselves and of the country generally.

Plate 6 'District Officer's House, Mempakul', photographer unknown.
Source: Sabah Museum, Sabah, Malaysia.

Chapter VI.
Up the River Kinabatangan.

The launch "Sabine."—Bahalla.—The Mumiang.—Mangrove swamps.—Batu Tummungong cave.—Its legend.—Melapi.— Bilet.—Wealthy natives.—Perils of birdsnesting.—Conferring a patent of nobility.—Sebongan.—Crocodiles.—Wild animals.— Orang-utans.—Lamag.—Rhinoceros for dinner.—A river flood.— Crocodile steaks.—Crocodile hunting.—Our Noah's ark.—Miss Champaka's wooing.—Reluctance of dogs to swim rivers.—A proboscis monkey's dilemma.—Sandflies.—Ordeal by boiling water.—Short of food.—Replenishing the larder.—The gymnura.—Spiny rats.—Toiling through mud-banks.

The following is an account of another journey up country:

We left Elopura in a houseboat named the "Waterlily" in tow of the Government steam launch "Sabine." The "Waterlily" is a boat built on the Shanghai houseboat model, her main cabin being of fair size. She boasts, besides, of a pantry, and has accommodation of a very limited kind at the stern for the crew and servants, where is also fitted up a fireplace for cooking, designed on a most primitive plan. In each bow there is a big projecting goggle eye, the boat having been made by a Chinese carpenter, who held the theory, like the rest of his race, that if at night "no got eye, no can see." We took a sufficient supply of loose planks to lay across the cabin from locker to locker, on which at nights we had our bed arranged, with a mosquito curtain suspended from nails in the roof.

Our intention was to ascend the Kinabatangan, one of the finest rivers in North Borneo, from the trade of which, augmented by that of the Labuk, situated to the north of Sandakan Bay, the town of Elopura has, up to the present time, owed its prosperity.

The first point of interest we passed was the island of Bahalla, whose richly coloured and precipitous sandstone cliffs rise to a height of 600 ft. above a white sandy beach, with here and there a pretty tree-surrounded cove and a fisherman's hut, built on piles over the sea, to complete as peaceful and charming a scene as can be imagined. Then followed a two hours' sea passage, at the end of which time we reached the Mumiang mouth of the Kinabatangan, the nearest entrance to the river from Elopura. For some twenty-five miles further down the coast one mouth succeeds another, the whole forming a great network of waterways, by means of which this fine river discharges itself into the sea, the water frequently being fresh or brackish for a mile or so outside. The Mumiang entrance resembles a great bay or inlet, some two miles broad and several miles long, into which numerous small streams empty themselves, the whole forming a most puzzling place for an inexperienced navigator to find himself in, all the surrounding swamps being thickly fringed with mangrove trees, so that one stream has no distinguishing features from another.

The mangrove swamps being passed, the nipa swamps succeed. From the bark of the mangrove, valuable dyeing and also tanning extract is obtained: whilst to the nipas, which in their growth much resemble gigantic ferns, we are indebted for our housebuilding materials; of them are made attaps for roofing, and kadjangs for the walls of our bungalows. Twenty-five miles of this monotonous scenery have to be passed before we reach the true forest-covered banks of the river, and we then have to steam another thirty miles or so ere reaching the first village. Before arriving at Melapi, we were called upon to sacrifice at the Batu Tummungong caves, the small entrance to which is decorated by numberless offerings in the shape of tiny flags of white and red cloth, stags' antlers, packets of rice, pieces of dried fish, small bundles of Chinese tobacco, incense sticks, and all sorts of odds and ends placed there by travellers. There is a story connected with these caves, but it is not a satisfactory one, as it appears to have no proper beginning, and ends in nothing particular. A party of brothers are supposed to have gone into the cave to sleep, when, for reasons unexplained, the rock at the entrance slowly closed down and shut them in, and it is to their imprisoned spirits that the offerings are made, in order that the fates may be propitious to the travellers who place them at the shrine. The scenery at this particular spot is lovely; a high sandstone bluff juts sharply on to the river, the top of it crowned with fine forest trees, and its face clothed with rich vegetation, amongst which spread great palm-shaped ferns, with fronds often 8 ft. long. There are no villages below Melapi, owing to the fear the natives used to have of the pirates who ravaged the coast line and drove all the more peacefully disposed people far up into the interior; and though this state of affairs has within the last ten years been put an end to, the natives have not yet ventured nearer the mouths of the rivers. As to Melapi, it is nothing better than a collection of tumble-down old shed-like houses, with a few cocoanut trees and bananas here and there. There being nothing to detain us at this place, we steamed on to the next village that night.

Bilet is a much more imposing and prosperous looking village, being inhabited by the Gomanton birds'-nest collectors, which caves yield a yearly revenue of $25,000, and make the owners so rich that they are able to buy anything they want or desire. In the old days they used to spend their surplus money in purchasing gongs, brass trays, basins, kettles, and boxes, native cannon manufactured at Brunei, and such like articles, which it was their custom to hide or bury in the forest, fearing lest, by keeping too much wealth in their houses, they might provoke the attacks of hostile tribes. The two yearly collections of birds'-nests used to be attended by a motley crowd of several hundred persons, who picked up a living in miscellaneous ways, such as cake-selling, coatmaking, peddling in all its branches, and begging. All these persons used to get big pickings, as the collectors were most prodigal with their wealth. A bundle of Chinese tobacco, worth 25 cents, would be exchanged for four catties of nest, worth $1 per catty; salt fish, value 12 cents per catty, was exchangeable for an equal weight of nest; and so on. One amongst other cave customs was, that if a person below called out "forfeit," the collector above had to throw down a nest, so that by these means alone the hangers-on made a good living.

Collecting birds' nests is a very hazardous occupation, the rattan ladders being in some instances 200 ft. long. As the caves are dark, it is necessary to use lights, and candles made of beeswax are employed, as ordinary wax or composite candles injure the nests should the wax fall on them. In the Gomanton caves both white and black nests are obtained, the former worth $8, and the latter $1 per catty – a catty equals $1\frac{1}{3}$ lb. The swiftlets which make the nests are of two kinds, the one which makes the black nest having a slightly larger head than the other. I do not know whether this fact is scientifically known.

The head man of the village was absent on a pilgrimage to Mecca, and had taken his family with him. The No. 2 man, my husband had authority to confer a title upon; so early next morning, all the inhabitants having been summoned, the governor's titah (or letters patent of nobility) was read by W. This done, there followed much banging of cannons and guns; some of the former refused to go off, however, and recourse had to be made to red-hot pieces of iron to the touch holes. Having safely passed through this ordeal, we steamed off on our up-country journey, and after passing a few groups of houses, near Bilet, hardly to be dignified with the term of villages, no other houses were seen all day.

Towards evening we reached Sebongan, 120 miles up stream. This point is tidal limit. There are now no houses at this place, the people having deserted it and moved nearer Bilet, owing to the number and ferocity of the crocodiles hereabout. Altogether over thirty individuals have been devoured by these awful brutes, and some of the accounts are very harrowing; but, with the usual apathy of the Malay nature, no attempts at reprisals were made.[14] The story runs that it was in consequence of a feud between the chief of the village, Pangeran Amai, and the crocodiles, that they were so bloodthirsty, he having in his youth sworn that he hoped he might be devoured by a crocodile if a statement he made was not true, well knowing that he was swearing falsely. The curious point of the tale is that, after the villagers had all moved down to Bilet, Pangeran Amai went to the Mumiang to collect nipas for roofing his new houses, and whilst there, was dragged out of his boat at night by a huge crocodile, and was never more seen again, although there were six or seven other men in the same boat.

The deserted fields and gardens here, being now covered with grass, afford food for large numbers of deer, bison (Bos banting), rhinoceros, and elephants. We saw the footprints on the muddy banks where one of the latter animals had landed after a swim across the river. On a former occasion on this spot my husband, having failed to come up with a herd of about forty elephants, was returning through the forest, when his men discovered some orang-utans sitting in a tree. He himself objects to shoot these animals, but the men began firing at them before he could stop them. The female, with a little one clinging to her, made off into the forest; but, being wounded, stopped in a high tree. Hearing a rustling behind him, he turned round and saw the male animal coming to his wife's assistance, although it clearly understood the danger, and was in fact shot by the men – a sad sacrifice to conjugal affection.

Early the next morning we arrived at Lamag, having passed through nearly sixty miles of tropical forest without seeing a single house, although if the country were China it would support hundreds of thousands of people, possessing as it does all the necessary elements for the support of a large population.

Having reached this place (Lamag), we sent the "Sabine" back, as we intended making a long stay, and, furthermore, proposed continuing our journey into the far interior when W. had finished his work at this place. There is a large native village here, and we saw a good deal of the people. On the day we arrived the natives had killed a rhinoceros, which their dogs had brought to bay when out pig-hunting. The men went in with their spears and killed it. The Lamagites, not being Mohamedans, do not scruple to eat anything that offers – snakes, monkeys, &c. – so they regarded the rhinoceros as affording an opportunity for a big feast. They offered W. a cut of steak, which he accepted, and ordered to be cooked for dinner, to my disgust. He protested that it was very good eating, and was something like pork and venison; but I declined to try it – indeed, I did not like to use the knives, forks, or plates for some days afterwards. Our cook,

Lam Chong, a Chinaman, bought the animal's small horn for five bundles of tobacco, as his countrymen prize all manner of strange and curious things as medicine, and no doubt he made a good profit over the transaction when he returned to Elopura. I possess one valued at $25.

There was with us Mr. A., a naturalist, whose cook was provided with a camp oven; so he and our cook used to have great baking matches, preparing and subsequently baking bread on a sandbank. One night the river rose nearly twenty feet, submerging the said sandbank. We usually lay at anchor in mid-stream, but on this and some other occasions, after heavy rains in the mountains of the interior, we had to haul our boat close in to the bank, to prevent ourselves being carried away by the big floating logs which swirled past us in numbers.

At this place the natives very wisely turn the tables on the crocodiles, preferring to eat them rather than be eaten by them. No less than sixty-seven had been caught in the preceding twelve months, some of very large size, and nearly 20 ft. long. I first found out that the natives had acquired a taste for crocodile flesh in the following way: At daybreak one morning the orderly came and called my husband, saying there was a big wild pig on the river bank close by. He got up immediately, and shot it from the boat. Having consequently a large supply of fresh meat, and knowing that the natives at this place would be glad of some, I, seeing a long dug-out canoe making its way up the river, hailed the occupants, intending to give them a portion of poor piggy. As they came alongside, the man in the bow put his head in at one of the cabin windows, and asked if we would like some "ekan besar" (big fish). An instant later, to my intense surprise, I found the "big fish" he offered was nothing else than crocodile. They had just captured it, and had hewn it into great steaks. This culinary delicacy we politely declined. The brute must have been about 12 ft. long; its skull is now in the Sandakan Museum. The mode of capturing these creatures is by firmly driving two stout but pliable poles into the river bank, and tying them together. To the lower one is attached a long single rattan, at the end of which half a dozen lines are made fast to a short stout stick to which is bound a dead monkey, or other such bait. A crocodile, however large, once swallowing this, and getting the stick crossways in his stomach, cannot drag away the apparently weak sticks, and is found and secured by the men when they go round to examine the lines.

As the accommodation for our boatmen was very limited, some of them made an upper storey on the roof of the boat. They bound poles to the sides of the boat with rattan, and then covered in the framework with kadjangs made of the ever useful nipa palm. In this country one never seems to be at a loss for this sort of thing. Rattans are always to be found close to hand, and, when split up into lengths, answer all the purposes of rope or string. Saplings abound everywhere, so that if you provide yourself before starting on your travels with a kadjang or two, you can make a snug enough little hut on very short notice. Our boat, when this addition had been made, looked like a big edition of a child's Noah's ark; however, she answered her purpose, and everyone on board, though packed like sardines in a tin, was now able to find a comfortable corner.

Amongst other bicharas – signifying in this instance a slave case – demanding W.'s attention, was that of a slave woman, rejoicing in the name of Champaka. "Champaka" is the name of a very sweet-smelling flower. Natives in this part of the world, and especially Sooloos sometimes give their children very odd names. For instance, I have known a man called "Ular" (snake); another, "Ubi" (potato); and another, "Kalug" (worm). But to return to Miss Champaka, who had run away from her mistress; she was not quite so youthful as she had been, and doubtless she thought it high time she got settled in life; so, the opportunity offering, she ran away with one of the river traders, to ask help from my husband. Her mistress followed her down to Lamag a day or two afterwards, accompanied by her daughter Fatima. Both these ladies were resplendent in silks of all hues of the rainbow – yellow silk trousers (Sooloo women, like Chinese women, always wear trousers); short emerald-green jackets, with exceedingly tight and long sleeves, that must be most uncomfortable to wear and difficult to get on and off; and to complete their costumes they wore the usual native garment, the sarong, dyed in a peculiar patchy way in dabs of magenta, yellow, green, and orange, hanging from their right shoulder, and partially concealing their forms. These aristocratic ladies wept copiously at losing their handmaiden, for, after a long and solemn bichara, Champaka was declared a free woman, and shortly afterwards married the man of her choice.

For three days a native dog wandered up and down the river bank, howling in a most distressing manner. He looked lean and miserable at first, and seemed to be growing hourly thinner; it was quite evident that he wished to cross the stream to get back to his home, and to this end we sent help on two occasions, but, not knowing the men or the boat, he refused assistance. No doubt he was taken out hunting by his owners and lost in the forest. All the native dogs are clearly alive to the danger of venturing into the rivers, and never do so unless under great excitement. At last the poor animal was driven to such straits that he cunningly made his plans, and when a large log came floating down nearer to the bank than usual, plunged into the stream, swam to it, and got upon it, and so was assisted some yards further across the river; then, finding the log was drifting too far down, he again jumped into the water, striking out bravely for the shore, when he arrived safely in a very short time.

A somewhat similar case occurred a day or two later, the animal in distress this time being a proboscis monkey, nearly 4 ft. high. This odd and dissipated looking old gentleman we discovered sitting on a post hanging over the water. It was clear that he also could not make up his mind to trust himself to the dangers of the river. He sat there cogitating for some time with a most melancholy expression on his queer face, his big red flabby nose, nearly two inches long, adding to his droll expression. As after a long time no help offered, he determined to plunge in, and in due time, although the current was flowing rapidly and he had to exert his full strength, he safely reached the opposite bank.

Every evening at sundown we were much tormented by the myriads of sandflies that swarmed about us; their bite is very irritating for a short time, the irritation returning again after a lapse of twenty-four hours. It was lucky that they did not trouble us for long; they cleared away after an hour's sport, to leave us in peace until the same hour the following evening.

Whilst taking our coffee one morning, we heard a great shouting and calling in the forest. W. sent to inquire the cause, and was informed that the ordeal by hot water was being undergone by a man who refused to acknowledge a debt. This test was perfectly voluntary. It appears that this method of settling disputes is often resorted to by natives. When these men came out of the forest, my husband called for them, wishing to personally inspect the hands that had been in the boiling water; they did not seem any the worse for it, and we do not know how the matter was managed; but, at any rate, the debtor was quite satisfied, for he told W. so. When the man's hand is in the hot water he relieves his feelings by loudly calling on Heaven to help him, and bear witness to the truth of his statements.

Owing to some mismanagement at Sandakan, our supplies of food were not sent forward to us, and we were left almost without "chow-chow." We could not look to the natives for much, sweet potatoes being the most substantial part of their diet, and such delicacies as crocodile steak, monkey stew, and snake pie, not being much to our taste. They rear no fowls for food, although they keep a few, and if they happen to have a few eggs they hoard them up until they are bad. On this occasion, hearing we were short of food, one of the principal villagers brought us an offering of four eggs, which we had boiled for breakfast; on opening them with hopeful expectation, we were, as usual, doomed to find them all uneatable.

We now had recourse to trapping. We set one of the men to make "jarrets," or hedges formed of branches and leaves, with gaps at intervals, each gap being supplied with a noose. These traps were visited twice daily, and sometimes yielded us a mousedeer, no bigger than a hare, a plump partridge of gorgeous plumage, or a lovely fire-back pheasant; but, sad to relate, more often it was a civet cat, a huge monitor lizard (here called iguana), or a sort of skunk that was trapped; whilst sometimes, when something good for the pot had been noosed, one of the uneatable creatures had been beforehand with us, and all that was left was a handful of feathers. Our larder was so reduced that we were at last obliged to make our breakfast, tiffin, and dinner off sweet potatoes, and the men were almost as badly off as ourselves, for their rice was almost all finished.

Amongst other curious creatures caught in the traps was a gymnura, a little white creature not much bigger than a guinea-pig, with a pig-like face and a bare rat-like tail. I believe no specimen of this animal has ever been imported into England, for the reason that the smell they emit is insufferable, and hangs about for such a long time; it is so overpowering, that I have been once or twice awakened from a sound sleep owing to one of these animals having simply passed below the house. Another curious creature caught was a prickly rat; it appeared to be a true rodent, but in place of hair was provided with little quills like a hedgehog. Little squirrels no bigger than mice were common in this locality.

At last the fresh stores which we had been expecting arrived, and we were then able to resume our journey. From this point our progress was very slow and most difficult, for our unfortunate crew had to tow our boat. The banks of soft black mud were cut across by numerous side streams and ditches. Along these slippery banks the men plunged wearily hour after hour – now in the water, now out, wet to the skin all day, with a blazing tropical sun pouring down upon them always at the least ankle-deep in the black, holding slime, and often sinking up to their knees. Yet there was never a murmur from any one of them, but they toiled along bravely and cheerily, changing gangs once in two hours. It was dreadfully unhealthy work, and we were very anxious about them. I do not think that in any other country one could have found such good-tempered and ready workers.

CHAPTER VII.
UP THE RIVER KINABATANGAN – (CONTINUED.)

Forest scenery over-rated.—Orchids.—Deserted gardens.—
Mungalis trees.—Bees' nests.—Blut.—Utu's house.— Champaka's
ladies.—Wild cattle.—Karangans, Malubuk River.— Quarmote
River.—Alexandra Falls.—Sonepis.—Tunbunwahs.—Tungaras.—
Native costumes.—Tobacco growing.—Summungup.—A revolting
custom.— Kinabalu the Borneo Valhalla.—Boats of the Sick
Spirits.—Domingol.—Lanteens.—Reception at Domingol.—
Establishing a Fair.—Cotton.—Karamoork river.—Frightened
children.—A main balugsi.—River Trade.—Further up the river.—
A durian feast.—Native mode of climbing trees.—Sundyaks.—The
river shallows.—Our return journey.—Malay traders.—Native
sloth.—Deer shooting.—Home again.

The usual accounts of tropical scenery are much overdrawn, so far as my experience extends; at any rate, with regard to the number of flowers to be met with. As a rule, the forest itself is one uniform dark green. Orchids are often to be seen; but their flowers are rarely conspicuous. There are, of course, exceptions, but they grow so high up in the forks of the trees that unless the tree is felled or a ladder made there is no getting them, climbing being practically impossible, for the great forest trees grow from 100 ft. to 150 ft. before they spread out a single branch in their search for light and air, their trunks being as straight as the columns of a cathedral aisle. On the river bank, however, one tree was often seen which proved an exception to this rule, this being doubtless the season for its blooming; rising to a height of 30 ft. or so, it was smothered in flowers of a bright lilac hue, and looked not unlike a rhododendron.

As we glided along we noticed many charming little patches of park-like scenery – places once under native cultivation, but now deserted and become grass land, which afford food to numerous deer and wild cattle, that make these pretty peaceful glades their feeding grounds. One could not help indulging in a desire to pitch one's tent and make a garden in one of these inviting spots.

The most noticeable tree in the forest is the mungalis, with its smooth white trunk, which springs straight up, towering high above all others before it spreads out its branches. For some reason or other, the wild bees that abound in this country seem to have a predilection for these trees, and sometimes one may count as many as twenty and even thirty bees' nests hanging from the branches of a single tree. The natives rarely exert themselves to obtain the wax, though it has a good market value, whilst the honey is simply wasted altogether.

On and on we went, wearily and slowly, our boat-men always good-tempered, and ready to make the best of a bad situation, never a grumble, never a murmur, making fun of each other when a companion sank to his armpits in soft ooze, pulling and tugging and laughing and swimming by turns. We passed no houses; we met no boats for days, except at a small village called Blut. In this campong there is only one decent house, but we found the Utu, proprietor, at home, who showed us his new domicile with great pride. He had recently paid Elopura a visit, and had become inspired with a desire to possess a better abode than his neighbours, so had erected one on the Sandakan model. This man had a wonderful tale about a coal mine, which W. promised to inquire further about on the first possible occasion.

Champaka's mistress and her two daughters live here – ladies of quite the highest aristocracy of the country, the same persons who visited us during our stay at Lamag in gorgeous array of purple, scarlet, green, and gold. Their home, however, we found to be a most wretched shanty, in which it was barely possible for them to stand erect, and so old and dilapidated that in wet weather the rain must have poured in upon them like water through a sieve. The ground underneath the house (for all houses in this country are built on piles) was in a most horrible and unsanitary condition, being wet with green slime, and all the refuse from the house – fish scrapings, potato parings, and everything else – being got rid of through the open flooring above, and had putrified and created a most evil smell; yet here were these people living above in utter unconcern, just as though deprived of the senses of sight and smell. It is needless to say I did not venture into this shed to return the owner's visit.

My husband went out shooting at dusk in some large fields prettily dotted here and there with trees and clumps of feathery bamboo. Whilst trying to stalk a deer that was uttering its sharp, loud cry, in walked a herd of wild cattle or buffaloes, which rushed off again with a noise like a charge of cavalry; but, unfortunately, owing to the falling night, and the moon not being up, he could not see to take aim.

Above Blut the river gets much swifter, and pebbly shallows occur, called *karangans* up which our crew had great difficulty in dragging the boat, the water rushing and splashing amidst the stones and rocks, and eddying round the bodies of the men, who were all in the water, hauling away with all their strength at two ropes, one from either bow, and fending us off from the rocks. On the third day from Blut we passed the Malubuk, a river with a mouth nearly fifty yards broad, but quite uninhabited. On the evening of the fourth day we reached the Quarmote, a fine stream, whose head waters rise far away in the interior. No Europeans have ever been up this river, which has a very strong and rapid current; four days' journey up it are Alexandra Falls, a fine cascade, said to descend forty yards – the entire river, in fact, rushing over rocks into a basin below.

Proceeding on our way up the Kinabatangan, which did not perceptibly decrease in width or volume, we soon arrived at a village called Sonepis, and from this time forward were never long without seeing houses. The people inhabiting this district are known as Tunbunwahs; the majority of whom are not Mohammedans, and consequently do not regard pigs as unclean beasts. Pigstyes, therefore, are often to be seen below their houses or in their gardens; these pigs are fattened up from time to time for their high feasts and holidays. The Mohammedan religion is fast gaining ground in the centre of Borneo however, and soon there will be very few people left who are not followers of the Prophet; but the Tunbunwahs find the necessity of doing away with their pig feasts a great stumbling block.

At this place we saw some Tungaras, whose proper district is up the Quarmote, a mild wilder race than the Tunbunwahs. Hearing they were here, W. sent to call them; but, as the men were afraid to come themselves, they sent a deputation of their women. I think we were the first Europeans they had ever seen; at any rate, they had never seen a white woman before. We regaled these persons with very sweet tea and sugared biscuits, presenting them on their departure with gifts of tobacco (for all native women enjoy cigarettes), some matches, which they highly prize – their usual mode of obtaining lights and fire being by means of a bamboo, bit of pith, and a broken piece of pottery – as well as some salt fish and rice.

I am unable to say that these Tungara ladies could boast of great personal attractions, when judged by our western standard of beauty. They load their bodies with all manner of ornaments, chiefly coils of brass wire, which they twist into wide waistbands, bangles for arms and ankles, also necklaces and ear-rings. One woman wore a kind of coronet formed of beads and wire, which hung in a sort of fringe over her forehead; tassels of beads also hung suspended from her ears, and her fingers were adorned with many rings. As for her coiffure, it was a sort of chignon at the back, puffed and padded with a handful of dried grass.

Further up the river we saw some nice tobacco growing amongst the paddi. The leaves were very fine and large. The natives do not attempt to ferment it, but simply dry it, cut it up small, and use it in their pipes or rolled into cigarettes, the covers of which are thin young leaves of the nipa palm. No doubt in days to come this will be a very prosperous tobacco growing district.[15]

Our boat-boys, with the usual patience characteristic of the Malay race, used to constantly devote their spare time to fishing, with but very poor results. One night, however, they met with unusual luck, and returned to the houseboat with two pail-fulls of beautiful silvery fish, off which we all feasted the next day.

For the next few days our journey was very tedious and uneventful. One gets tired even of admiring this fine river, and the unbroken line of forest trees grows dreadfully monotonous. Villages, however, occurred much more frequently than they did below Quarmote, and we stopped at each one, as there were bicharas and quarrels to settle at nearly all of them. At one place a small chief came forward to make a request. The weather had been unusually dry, and as a means of inducing rain – for need of which the crops were suffering much – this wicked old wretch asked that he might be allowed to summungup one of his slaves. Summungupping is a most revolting and barbarous custom, which the natives of the interior would like to carry into effect if permitted to do so. It is needless to say that this request was promptly refused, and the man was cautioned not to pursue such practices in future. The ceremony of summungupping is as follows: Having obtained a slave for the purpose, the unfortunate being is bound with ropes and tied to a post: thereupon all the villagers approach armed with spears, which they thrust a short distance into the slave's body, at the same time requesting him to convey messages to their deceased relations on Kina Balu. (I may here explain that Kina Balu, the largest mountain in the B.N.B. Company's territory, represents the heaven of these people. The good individuals who die ascend the rocky heights and live in joy at the summit: whilst the bad ones, ceaselessly and ineffectively try to scramble up its cold and rugged sides to the abode of bliss above.)

Whilst continuing our way up stream we saw a miniature house floating down towards us. It was gaily decorated with flags, and was fitted on to a lanteen or raft. I wished to have it, but the boatmen refused, in their usual courteous Malay fashion, to interfere with it, explaining that someone in a village above must be ill, and that this little house had been launched on the river in the hope that the illness would be floated away in it, and the boatmen were afraid that if they took it, the sickness, which they imagined to be on board it, would attack us or some member of our party.

At a point near here we found a boat full of men awaiting us, sent down to assist us by the thoughtful kindness of Pangeran Dermatuan, who had received news of our approach by Panglima Banjer, whose boat being a swift gobang or dug-out canoe, travelled faster than our heavy houseboat. The river from this point was more thickly populated. At Termoy there were some sago and cocoanut palms growing, almost the first we had seen. The same day we arrived at Domingol, our place of halt.

Domingol is charmingly situated: the first sight we caught of it as we rounded a bend of the river much surprised and pleased us. Panglima Dermatuan's house, a large and roomy structure, stands in a commanding position at the point of a promontory surrounded by cocoanut and other fruit trees, with the B.N.B. Company's flag flying above it. The surrounding country is cleared and under cultivation for a comparatively long distance back from the river banks. Here and there, dotted about amongst paddi and sweet-potato fields, are the houses of Panglima Dermatuan's followers, each crowning a little hill; whilst, forming a background to this rural and peaceful scene of contentment and plenty, rose in the far distance ranges of hills and mountains all forest clad to their summits.

On the river were many lanteens (rafts) completing their cargoes of rattans. In some cases quite large houses were erected upon these lanteens, with verandahs in front. I should think it must be most comfortable to travel in this way. Unfortunately they can only be used to float down stream, as it would not be possible to get them past karangans or up rapids. There was also quite a little fleet of traders' boats. All these elements afforded a very attractive and gratifying picture, and testified to the wealth of the surrounding forests.

The Panglima received us with much banging of native cannon, and escorted us to his house, in which, on an elevated platform, he had arranged a seat of honour gorgeously draped with silks of all the colours of the rainbow. A number of the chief villagers collected and squatted round about the edge of the platform, and certain matters were discussed, to be gone into more fully on a later occasion.

Not only from a distance was Domingol attractive, but, unlike most native villages, we were surprised and glad to find that Panglima Dermatuan induces his people to devote some attention to sanitary matters, so that the open spaces below the houses here are all kept clean and tidy. I think very special praise is due to the Panglima, for it is solely in consequence of his example that these people keep their houses so well, as Domingol is situated in the heart of Borneo, and no European influence is brought directly to bear upon them.

There being a fairly large campong here, and the Malay traders enjoying a little recreation, the male portion of the inhabitants usually collected on a small plat of an evening to play at ball – "main-raga" they call it. This game is not played as in England, with the hand or a bat, but the ball, which is a light one made of rattan, is kept in motion by kicks given by the inner side of the ankle of the right foot, and much skill is shown in keeping it in the air. Such persons amongst the circle of players as aspire to be dandies airily wave bright-coloured silk handkerchiefs in their right hands.

At Domingol we found some very fine cotton growing, which no doubt would prove a very profitable article of commerce if more largely cultivated.

Thinking it might give an impetus to trade, my husband declared that a market should be held beneath the trees near the Panglima's house, and messengers were sent to ask people to come from all the nearest villages, and bring with them whatever they had to sell, on a certain given day. Wishing to make the affair a success, amongst other things we instigated an old Sooloo woman to make cakes, advancing her sufficient capital for the purchase of the necessary rice-flour, sugar, and cocoanuts. She sat up most of the night making her bake-meats, and on the market morning had a supply of cakes of many kinds and shapes, but all, I believe, of much the same flavour, which attracted many customers. She and her cakes were, in fact, the chief feature of the market, which, unfortunately, went off rather flatly, the natives on the first occasion scarcely understanding what was going to occur.

One evening we made a short trip up the Karamoork river in a large canoe, manned by our eight boat-boys. They made a smart little crew in their uniform-white trousers, blue blouses with sailor collars, red dustahs on their heads, and red sashes round their waists. As they rowed they sang Malay boat-songs, keeping time to the splash of their paddles. Houses and gardens line the banks of the Kinabatangan on both sides above Domingol; but the Karamoork, which is a tributary, is very thinly inhabited, owing to its nearness to a head-hunting tribe on the north side, who not many months before had come over and taken twenty-two heads, mostly those of women and children. As we rounded a bend of the river, we saw several little boys enjoying an evening bathe. When they discovered us they roared lustily, rushing off like lightning to hide themselves, thinking doubtless that we were a party of the dreadful head-hunters. A little distance further up we landed, and paid a visit to a house standing in a large potato field. W. recognized the proprietor. It seems that he cut down and killed a man leaving his wife's mosquito curtain. He afterwards travelled all the way to Elopura to report himself and be tried.

Circumstances, it proved, justified his conduct, so he was acquitted and sent back to his country. Being a strong-nerved man, he had been put in one of the farthest houses up the Karamoork.

On the night of the market at Domingol we were invited to be present at a "main-balugsi" given by the Panglima. From the time it began at about 8 p.m., until broad daylight the next morning, the dancing continued without intermission. Two or three men step out into the centre of the house, join hands in a circle, and commence to move round and round, chanting a dirge-like solo, the rest joining in the choruses. The songs are "topical" ones, referring to anything of local interest.

We were some days at Domingol, and had plenty of time to look about us and admire the fine plank walls the Panglima was putting round his house, and how his wife Fatima's paddy-planting prospered; besides which, there was a most important case brought into court, about one man's goats, who were accused of eating up another man's sweet potatoes, and many other matters of absorbing local interest.

The trading transactions which took place at Domingol were not insignificant. Having rattan-cutting rights on the Karamoork river, the Panglima was carefully preserving the rattans there, instead of allowing them to be exterminated by indiscriminate collection, as was the case in other parts of the river, and a constant and steady outflow of produce is the consequence. Every day a few bundles of rattans were added to the different traders' stocks, and placed on the lanteens, which, when full, are floated away down stream.

At last we proceeded on again, and ascended the Kinabatangan beyond its junction with the Karamoork. The river did not seem to get a bit smaller, but, although it was just as broad, we soon found it was not so deep, and some seven or eight miles above the Karamoork our progress was brought to a stop altogether by shallows up which the boat could not possibly pass. At this point we were, according to the map, over 1000 ft. above sea level in the boat, and in the centre of this part of Borneo.

The country was very nice; houses and gardens lined both sides of the river. A "main-balugsi" was held in our honour in the house opposite which we had moored our boat, and was attended by a rather larger number of girls than usual, all dressed in the most gorgeous silks of all the hues of the rainbow. These Tunbunwah girls were rather good-looking. Next day W. went on an exploring trip up the Bod Tinkah Hills, the first European who had ascended them. His intention was to try and find a flat of land, at an elevation of 2000 ft. or so, on which a house could be erected for the officer in charge of the district. The search was not altogether successful, as the ridges were too narrow and steep; but a heavy thunderstorm, attended by a deluging rain, drove the party back to the boat before their explorations were fully accomplished. In the course of their excursion they had come across a durian tree in bearing, and as this is a fruit I am very fond of, we went off in the afternoon to try and get some.[16] We found a few ripe ones on the ground which had fallen but our appetites were only tantalised by these, for the natives are equally fond of them, and assisted us at our feast. We tried to get some more, and a particularly well-built Sulu, the strong man of our crew, who said he should cry all night if he could not have a durian or two, volunteered to ascend the tree, which was about 4 ft. thick, and rose straight up for 100 ft. without putting out a single branch; there was, however, a smaller tree alongside it, by ascending which Magheer thought to get over into the branches of the durian. So up he went; but when about 30 ft. from the ground he disturbed a wasps' nest, and, roaring lustily, tumbled rather than climbed down to earth again. Not dismayed by this *contretemps*, however, another of our crew, a slight little fellow, who said he was impervious to wasp stings, essayed next. As he neared the nest he crept up so quietly and softly that his limbs were hardly seen to move, but some of the wasps came out, and he was stung half a dozen times, enduring the pain most stoically; but, after all, he had to return disappointed, for he could not reach across to the durian tree. He was determined, however, not to be beaten. We then summoned a lot of villagers to our aid, with a promise of a large gift of rice if they would get the durians; so, a larger party than ever, we started off again in quest of the much-coveted fruit early the next morning. The Sundyak (Sundyak is the general term in use for the Tunbunwahs, Romanows, and other neighbouring tribes) method of ascending trees is very curious. Appearing to regard the tree itself as one side of a ladder, they seek to fix the missing side to it, and place the rungs between the two. This they accomplish in the following manner: First of all, they cut a lot of wooden pegs about a foot in length, which they sharpen at one end. These are the rungs, the sharp end of one of which is driven into the tree about five feet from the ground. A pole some fifteen feet or so long is then tied securely to the outer end of the peg. At intervals of four feet or so apart two more pegs are driven into the tree, the workman ascending on the last peg driven in, when he fixes one above; and the pole being tied to each of these pegs, there is a ladder left below, 12 ft. long, to begin with. But the most puzzling part of the work now begins. It is all very easy to make the first part of the ladder, with the ground as a support for the first pole; but what support can there be for the second one up in the air? This problem, however, presents no difficulties to the

Sundyak's mind. He lashes some three feet of the bottom end of the next pole to the 3 ft. of the top end of the first one, and then, putting in his rung, ties the second stick to it, and, ascending as before, continues to lengthen his ladder indefinitely. This being accomplished, a second difficulty presented itself, for the tree was full of bull-headed black ants, which fastened with ferocity on everyone who went up; and after a dozen durians had been obtained from the lower branches, the men came out of the tree, declaring that they could not stand the bites of these dreadful ants. But again Mathassan, the slightly built boat-boy, came to the rescue, and, going up, did not leave the tree until he had thrown down the last durian. When he regained the ground he was perfectly black with ants, which had to be swept off him in handfuls. We all had a fine feast of durians, and returned to the boat happy.

My husband had intended to ascend to Penungah, the furthest inland of the Government stations, where there is a garrison of five men, who are considered quite sufficient to maintain order in that district; but the want of water in the river and the great karangans prevented it, for it was quite impossible to get our gobang past them (we had left our houseboat and migrated into a dug-out canoe, hoping by this means to be able to accomplish our purpose); so we had to return to our houseboat again after only a few hours' absence.

Penungah is quite a busy trading place as well as Government station. The Kinabatangan proper ends at this place, and divides into four rivers, all of them fairly well populated; so, from its central position, as population increases it is clearly destined to become a place of considerable importance in course of time. At present it is the point which most of the traders ascending the river make their goal. The mode of conducting trade in these parts is curious; three or four responsible Malays club together in Sandakan, and going to a Chinese shop, borrow goods to the value of about $500 or so, seldom giving anything in the way of security. Storing these goods in a long narrow canoe suitable for river work, they ascend the Kinabatangan, usually only making a stay of a day or two at the lower villages to rest, catch fish, or buy potatoes, as there is not much to do in the way of trade with these places, they being in touch with Sandakan itself, from which place they draw their own supplies. Farther up their stops at the different villages grow longer and longer as customers increase in numbers – one to buy a pair of Chinese trousers, another 6 yards of grey shirting, a third half-a-dozen cheap and gaudy plates, a fourth 10 lb. of salt, a fifth a brass box to hold his betel-nut appliances in, and so forth. Nearly all these things are sold on credit, the buyer promising to pay half-a-dozen bundles of rattans, a few catties of beeswax or indiarubber, or some other article of forest produce on the trader's return journey, but the mainstay of the trade is rattans. Proceeding from village to village in this way, it is usually eight or nine months before Penungah is reached, where a longer stay than ever is made, while the traders get rid of the balance of their stock at the best price they can. Penungah is a place flowing over with milk and honey, figuratively speaking – a fine and healthy climate, good soil, field produce (except rice) so cheap that it can be had for the asking, and fish plentiful. The traders while away their time attending "main-mains" (native dances) or solemn assemblages for reading the Koran at each other's houses, or sometimes making excursions to far-off villages to sell off any goods that hang on their hands.

When they propose to descend the river they make rafts of bamboo about 30 ft. across, and usually as broad, upon which they build a palm-leaf house. This raft they load up with whatever goods they have obtained by barter, and drop down from village to village, collecting their debts of kind as they go along, and in about a year from the time of their starting away they once more find themselves in Sandakan, with produce worth $1,000 or so, which they take to the shop of the Chinaman who originally fitted them out. After paying him off they usually have enough money left to divide $80 or $90 amongst themselves. There are, of course, no wages to pay, whilst as for food they have eaten very little besides sweet potatoes, tapioca, bananas, and other such things which the natives give them, and the fish they catch with their own cast nets; and this lazy existence exactly suits the calm and placid Malay character. The confidence with which the Chinese shopkeeper sees a gang of men taking away several hundred dollars' worth of his stock, disappearing with it for months up rivers or to far-off islands, is very remarkable, and is rarely abused.

The natives, too, pass a pleasant slothful existence; they know no want, and have very few cares; a very little labour in their fields and gardens yields them paddy, sweet potatoes, maize, pumpkins, cucumbers, and melons, bananas, and the like in larger quantities than they can consume; a week or two's forest produce collecting provides them with plenty of rattans and other things which they can barter for cloth, brass ware, and other small necessaries for their households. Their houses are usually fairly large and cool, and cost them nothing except labour; two or three broods of chickens pick up a living for themselves in the paddy fields; and the pigs, kept below the houses, get an armful of sweet potato tops flung to them once a day, whilst they in turn provide the chief joints, served up on high days and holidays; and dozens of big earthenware jars, the only things to which they attach any ideas of value, are stored away in every spare place. What more do these people want?

Not being able to go any farther, we at last pulled up our anchor and proceeded to float down stream, which was a most pleasant mode of progression. Seated upon deck in the cool of the evenings, we slowly and smoothly glided along, passing houses, gardens, fruit trees, grassy glades, clumps of feathery bamboo, with the soft winds murmuring in their leaves, and strips of forest now and then intervening; tying up at night to a tree in a covered bend of the river. We found that by proceeding in this manner we could shoot more game than in any other way; gliding noiselessly along we two or three times floated close to where deer were unsuspiciously nibbling the grass and leaves near the river bank, affording easy shots to W.'s gun, and their meat was a most welcome change of diet for our crew.

When still five or six days short of Sandakan, W. got ill, and I became most anxious to get him quickly home. Our men were very good; tying a rope from the large canoe to the houseboat, they towed us day and night without stopping, one half the crew relieving the other at stated intervals. By this means our return was much hastened, and in a very short time we arrived at Elopura, having made a very pleasant and interesting trip but for its unfortunate conclusion.

The healthy climate of Sandakan and fresh sea breezes, soon restored my husband, while as for myself I had been quite well the whole journey through.

CHAPTER VIII.
AMONG THE BULUDUPIES AND BAJOWS.

The Buludupies.—Former population.—Physical characters of the Buludupies.—Dr. Rey's researches.—Forest produce.—Trade with China.—Chinese settlers.—A change for the worse.—W.'s. arrival.—Sad decay of the native population.—Origin of the Buludupies.—Born of Satan.—Clever firemakers.—The Bajows coloured sails.—Sea gypsies.—Origin of the Bajows.—Legend of Ayesha.—Ibrahim's story.—Skill as fishermen.—Spearing fish.— The Balignini pirates.—Omaddas settlement.—Unpleasant experience.—Bajow raid on Bulungan traders.—Chasing the pirates.—Fired on by police.—Escape of the pirates.— Silam in a state of siege.—Native allies.—Threats from Omaddal.— Reinforcements sent for.—The women in the forest.—Arrival of S.S."Paknam".

In the early days before Europeans disturbed the semi-order that then existed Borneo was a fairly well populated and smiling rural country. Of the various tribes the Buludupies were one of the most flourishing. The character of the face of these people differs in some degree from that of the more typical Mongolian type, their eyes being so round and the bridge of the nose so developed, that Dr. Rey a French scientific man, who visited North Borneo in 1881 was inclined to think, that they were of semi-Caucasian ancestry. However this may be, in the times I write of, they inhabited the country from the Sugut on the North, to the Segama on the South; their fragile boats sailed about trading and fishing amongst the green islands that plentifully dot the shallows and ever-calm sea, their paddy fields were large, their orchards scattered over many thousands of acres, their young men could mount inside the steepest and slipperiest caves for birds nests, or the highest and thickest trees for beeswax, and to this tribe almost solely was confined the art of extracting from the tree the valuable barus camphor so highly prized in China. Their old men peacefully guided the affairs of the different villages, and in the mellow warmth of an ever-balmy climate, life glided tranquilly along. Then it was, that clumsy junks from Amoy running before the northerly monsoon came through the Philippine Islands to Sulu, and from then passing Tawi Tawi arrived on the Borneo coast dropping their goods as they went, crockery, ironware, silks and the like; and taking on board birdsnests, beeswax and rattans, cuttle fish, keema and trepang at the various islands they touched at on their way back.[17]

Junks at this time maintained a good trade with Brunei and other ports on the west coast, and Chinese traders settling down in many places married native girls and to a large extent mixed with the people of the country, infusing a good many Chinese customs and habits into their daily life, such as the wearing of large rings and circles of brassware, their liking for pork, and veneration for old jars and many others.

But a change was to come over this tribe as over all other things in the whole of Borneo. There was to be an end of the quiet, easy, slightly dreamy life under a pleasant warm sky, where the rich soil gave back a hundred fold the slightest attention paid to it, where the produce of the forest, of the birdsnest caves, or the rattan swamp were within easy reach, and were at once exchangeable for rich silks and other commodities from China. No longer were the heavy junks to come lazily down the Sulu seas, nor the Buludupies to cultivate their fields in peace. The only traders were to be Parang men, inhabitants of one of the fiercest districts of Sulu, but men with commercial instincts, capable of giving back blow for blow with the pirates; the population of whole districts was to disappear, and the land so late a smiling garden was to revert to dense jungle, tenanted only by the elephant and the orang utan.

When W. arrived in North Borneo, but a miserable remnant existed of what had been one of the most numerous and most prosperous tribes in Borneo. Of a mild and gentle disposition, they were particularly unfitted to struggle with the troublous times that arose, and were rapidly on the road to total extinction. Of all those inhabiting the Sandakan district, but seventeen adult males survived in villages up the Sigaliod river, and worried by the Sulus and almost driven to despair by repeated head-hunting raids, they were on the point of abandoning cultivation altogether when he came on the scene, and by intervening between them and the Sulus, gave them fresh courage and enabled them to gather for themselves the fruits of their own fields without seeing it seized under one pretext or another by hectoring Sulu chiefs.

They showed their appreciation of W. in various ways, and Ibrahim their chief in particular became a great crony of his, acting as his guide on hunting expeditions, instructing him in wood-craft and native agriculture, and telling him long legends about the country. Amongst other tales, he alleged that his tribe was descended direct from Satan, giving the following account of their ancestry.

Once upon a time, a certain old lady who had two daughters, wished to boil her rice but could not produce the light wherewith to kindle the fire. She then called upon her two daughters who also tried and failed, and she was very angry with them, which put one of them in such a passion that she ran off to a tree and offered to give herself to "Satan" if he would help her to produce fire, whereupon on trying again she struck a light easily. That night she disappeared. Three nights afterwards, the mother dreamed that if she went to a certain tree in the forest she would find her daughter, and upon doing so found her accordingly. In the course of time the girl gave birth to a son who was the ancestor of the Buludupies.

However all this may be, the fact remains that the Buludupies seem to have the knack of extracting fire from many most unpromising substances, and are never at a loss for a light for their cigarettes, even though they have no lucifer matches. Their usual way of producing fire is to take a piece of dry bamboo about $\frac{1}{3}$ of an inch thick, scrape it until they have produced a flocky substance, then with a little bit of broken pottery, a piece out of any old plate or tea-cup, held between their finger and thumb, holding some of the flock to the pottery with the thumb, they strike it smartly against the edge of the bamboo and a spark is produced which kindles the flock.

Many of the Buludupy women are quite fair, almost if not quite as white as Portuguese or Spaniards.

About the shores of these seas, small boats borne along by bright parti-coloured sails are frequently to be seen. Sometimes these sails are made of alternate blue and white stripes, sometimes red predominates, while occasionally they are a combination of red, white and blue. As a rule these are Bajow boats.

The Bajows or Sea gipsies are a strong muscular dark race, the darkest of all the Malay tribes. They have the appearance of having been pickled and preserved by the salt sea breezes which they love so well, and the hot direct rays of the brilliant tropical sun. The children of this tribe go about absolutely unclothed until an advanced age. They lead a free roving life in boats, here to-day, gone to-morrow, very rarely settle on the land, and when they do, always select lonely spots along the sea-shore: they are a reckless, feckless race, living from hand to mouth; they never think of planting anything and take flight like a flock of scared sea-birds on the slightest provocation.

The ancestry of the Bajows is somewhat doubtful. Certain it is that they are not true aboriginals of this part of Malayu, and an account of the conversion of the Kingdom of Brunei to Mahomedanism, taken from Brunei chronicles, (of which a vivacious account was given in the pages of "All the Year Round" a few years ago) probably supplies the clue as to their origin, corroborated as it is by a tale told by Ibrahim of the first appearance of the Bajows in these waters. It does not quite fit in with what the Bajows themselves say, without there is a place named Gorangtalo in Johore, as that (Gorangtalo) is where they claim to come from.

Once upon a time, so the story goes, a certain Sultan of Johore was the father of a beauteous daughter, bearing the style and name of Dayung Ayesha.[18] Glowing accounts of her charm of face and feature travelled to the distant courts of the Sultans of Brunei and Sulu, so that the Sultans of those kingdoms beyond the seas, desired much to obtain her for a bride. Her father naturally favoured the suit of the Sultan of Sulu (Sulu in those days being the most important state of the three, which account tallies very well with what we glean from other chroniclers who assign to the Sulu archipelago the seemingly incredible population of 200,000 persons). Dayung Ayesha herself meantime seems to have come more closely into contact with and lost her heart to the Sultan of Brunei, who we are told succeeded in surreptitiously visiting the Astana at Johore.[19] A day however arrived, when all preparations being completed, the obdurate father turning still a deaf ear to the prayers of his weeping daughter, compelled the lovely Ayesha to embark in a specially constructed boat and start for Sulu, attended by a fleet as convoy, and under the charge of many fighting men, to whose care she was particularly committed, to become the bride of the Sultan of Sulu. Soft and favouring winds filled the parti-coloured sails, and gently rippling waves bore the charming but still weeping princess safely across the intervening sea without incident, until the flotilla neared the shores of Borneo. No thought of surprise entered into the minds of the fighting men, her protectors, who lay lazily on the decks of the prahus, basking in the brilliant sunshine, chewing sirrih or meditatively rolling cigarettes.[20] But suddenly, when off their guard, and under cover of the falling night, a desperate onslaught was made by the Sultan of Brunei, who led a fleet to the attack, and a fight ensued. When the fight was at its fiercest, the Sultan himself, in a specially prepared and fast prahu, came alongside Dayung Ayesha's boat. She jumped on board, and leaving the two struggling fleets to fight it out, the loving couple rapidly disappeared into the night.

Next morning found the Johore fleet in a very unpleasant predicament. Bereft of their special charge, to return to Johore would be simply courting death at the hands of the enraged father. Very little better treatment could they expect if they went on to meet the disappointed Sulu Sultan, while they had just been fighting the fleet of the Sultan of Brunei, whose coast they were then off, so it would seem judging from the results (and always supposing that this series of tales is true), that they made over towards Celebes. But meeting strong winds they did not make much way; and, their stores exhausted, they had to take by force or otherwise pick up, as well as they could, such provisions as they were able; and finally became outcasts, or a species of Flying Dutchmen as it were, living by stealth, and in time carrying off young women for wives whenever they could catch them, every man's hand being against them. The weather-beaten boats, were replaced by smaller new ones, built by themselves in unfrequented places, mostly sandy islands, and gradually they degenerated into the Sea Gypsies they now are. On a few sandy undesirable islands they have settlements, but as a rule they prefer living on the water, each family in a boat to itself.

According to Ibrahim (and it is rather curious to get confirmatory evidence from such a quarter as this, as it is extremely unlikely that Ibrahim ever heard of the Dayung Ayesha and the matters in connection with her marriage) in the long past two large boats, much larger than the ones the Bajows now use (the theory being that there were two of the original Johore fleet), appeared off Bahala, and the Buludupies, whose main district in this immediate neighbourhood was then the Blocking, a river at the back of the Mumiang harbour, sent off some of their old men to parley with the strangers. This again, by the way, is quite characteristic of the Buludupies. The reception accorded to the unfortunate castaways by all other tribes in these waters, was of the " 'eave 'aalf a brick at 'is, 'ead" order, whereas the timid Buludupies, averse to the use of force, immediately begin to treat. The Bajows, finding what sort of folk they had to deal with, seem to have put on threatening airs; a compromise was arrived at, whereby the Buludupies agreed to retire into Sandakan Bay, resigning their foreshore rights, and the small birdsnest caves on Balhalla to the Bajows, who for their part agreed not to make any settlement on shore. This agreement, Ibrahim added, had been adhered to until quite recently.

They are, *par excellence*, the fishermen of this part of this world, seemingly half fishes themselves, their powers of swimming and diving are remarkable; they are the principal collectors of the sea-produce, shark's fins, beche de mer, keemah, tortoiseshell, turtle eggs and pearls. Their food includes all kinds of oysters, limpets, and such like creatures gathered upon the shores. So improvident are they, that I may cite as an instance, that once a Bajow, having received in barter for some find of extra value, more rice than he cared to carry in his boat, simply threw half of it away rather than be at the trouble of conveying it to a safe place.

They throw three-pronged fish-spears with great dexterity, and coasting in the shallows, a Bajow will secure at 50 or 60 feet distant a comparatively small fish, darting across the front of his boat, as adroitly as a sportsman will drop a pheasant, a wonderful feat considering that he has to allow not only for the pace the fish is swimming, but also the deflection caused by the refraction of water.

Owing to the nature of their surroundings the Bajows are of a lawless character. The far famed and greatly dreaded Balignini are one of their sub-tribes; these people were justly feared in all these waters on account of the systematic raids they used to make, not only on the tribes near home, but also to far distant countries, solely for kidnapping purposes; and all references to the annals of countries as far away as the Straits Settlements, Dutch Borneo, and Java bear testimony to their ferocity.

In but two or three places have the Bajows made proper settlements, one of these being the Omaddal district situated in the S.E. of our Territory. For long past these people have been in possession of the neighbouring seas, regarding as their lawful prey anything or anybody that came along their way. There are some thousands of them, a big, strong, bold, bronzed race, unscrupulous to a degree.

My experiences of them have been very unpleasant. On one occasion when W. was in charge of the Darvel Bay district, we came to close quarters with them; he was informed that a boatful of people coming up for trading purposes from Bulungan, had been captured while passing across their front; their goods seized and themselves sold as slaves. On hearing this, W., immediately sent down the steam launch to demand their release, and also the surrender of the men who had captured them. Knowing full well the desperate nature of the Omaddalites, he gave the Serang, (the man in charge of the launch) orders not to drop anchor or to let off steam, but to keep moving slowly about, in order that he should not be surprised by a sudden rush of boats, neither was he to allow any of the Bajows, except those he demanded, on board. Several of the captured people were handed over, but the boats and goods were retained, and the persons who had committed the act of piracy were declared not to be known, which was of course untrue, but naturally such desperadoes do not stick at a lie.

The real fact of the case became apparent soon after. It turned out that these particular persons had left Omaddal for Silam in their boats before the arrival of the launch, consequently they knew nothing of what had occurred, or of the "Sabine's" visit to their stronghold, or the rescue of the captured men and their removal to Silam. Accordingly, the day after the Bulungan people arrived in Silam, who should present themselves there but two Bajow boats, manned by the pirates, come to buy rice, &c., and little guessing what was in store for them, and also no doubt believing that their misdeed had not reached W.'s ears. However one of the kidnapped men happening to be sitting on the wharf at the time, and at once recognized his captors, and went without delay to the native magistrate to report the fact, who in his turn came to my husband for orders.

W. gave instructions to him to call out the police immediately, who were to hold themselves ready for further orders, while he himself went at once without delay to the wharf where the pirates were said to be. On arrival there, he found that they had already taken alarm, had flung down the bags of rice they had bought, and were paddling off in their two boats as fast as they could. In order to catch them, W. saw that immediate steps must be taken. Jumping into the first boat handy with two or three men he gave chase, – issuing at the same time orders for the proper row-boat to be brought round from the boat-house and manned with armed police.

W. was gaining on the pirates, who on their part, were dashing up the water with their paddles as they skimmed over the sea, when to his surprise the police on shore suddenly opened fire. By this time the news of what was occurring had spread from house to house like wild-fire, every man, woman and boy in the place who could find a weapon turned out and rushed off to the shore; Adasiah, the native magistrate's wife, came to me in wild disorder, her raven locks streaming in the breeze, a kris in her hand, to share in the matter. The scene of confusion that ensued can be imagined. Meanwhile the police rushed madly along the shore and continued to blaze away recklessly, regardless alike of friend and foe. The pirate boats bounded over the shimmering sea, the men paddling with the energy of despair, each vigorous stroke sending up a cloud of spray two or three feet high. While W. in his boat was rapidly gaining on them, I stood on the end of the wharf watching the chase, full of alarm as to what might happen next, for the stupid police still continued to fire as fast as they could recharge their guns. Suddenly one of the boats faltered, then the two closed up together, the men from one sprang overboard into the water, and quick as thought scrambled into the other, seized their paddles and rowed on with increased speed, the numbers of oars being now doubled.

The police all this time continued their mad course, rushing along the shore, taking pot shots as they went, and the row-boat being in the line of fire, the balls were whizzing all about it; one of them carried away the dustah, or head cloth, of one of W's men as he sat beside him.

After a mile or so had been covered, a mangrove swamp luckily prevented the police from further persuing their reckless course, and W. was left to continue the chase by himself.

Pursuer and pursued were progressing at equal speed, and W. was so close that he was able to put two or three shots through their sails without fear of hitting any of the occupants. Finding that they could not hold out much longer, the pirates rapidly pulled in towards the mangrove swamp, jumped into the shallow water and disappeared amongst the tangled net-work of the roots. W. followed them a short distance through the mud, but could not get up to them as it was fast growing dark. He could easily have shot them while still in the boat had he so thought fit. He started back with one boat, picking up the forsaken one half way back, when he discovered a great splash of blood at the stem. On arriving at Silam examination showed that out of 112 cartridges expended, the two boats had been hit five times.

An inquiry into the conduct of the police resulted in them all being fined, and the Sergeant in charge disrated.

It soon became apparent that we were in rather an unpleasant predicament. These occurrences had been seen by other boats which had not yet reached Silam, and which promptly returned to Omaddal carrying the news of what had happened. A declaration of war from Omaddal was the immediate consequence.

W. sent out boats to try to pick up the men in the forest, but so did the Bajows, who found and carried them off, minus the one, who shot in the back, had tumbled overboard, and whose body was never seen again, having been probably devoured by sharks.

The natives at the upper end of the Bay rallied round us to a man, Panglima Laut in particular coming in with all the men he could collect, to our aid, while Pangeran Amas and Dato Asivee also lent their boats and men to act as scouts.

The police force consisted of thirteen men, one of whom, a big black Somali took the opportunity of going mad, and required the constant attention of two others to control him. The sergeant could only speak Hindoo and Chinese, neither language being of much use under the circumstances; about half the rifles were defective, and what ammunition remained, was most of it bad; and as by this time messages of an unpleasant character still continued to arrive, it will be understood that our position was not exactly an enviable one, more especially as the fort was not calculated to withstand the rush of such a number of desperadoes as was threatened to be brought against it.

Amongst the characteristic messages were such as these – "That they (the Omaddal people) intended to come and pick up our heads as they would gather shells on the seashore." "That they would sweep the ground with the carcase of Dato Gumbah (the native magistrate) and holy stone it with the head of Panglima Laut.'

W. had sent off the "Sabine" with the news of these occurrences, at the same time asking for aid, while we waited in daily expectation of an attack.

The fort was strengthened in a hasty and rough manner, a palisading of stout forest-sticks was put round it, and broken bottles were planted on the grassy embankment surrounding it; the police were put on duty all night and allowed all day for rest. A cordon of Eraan boats acted as scouts behind the islands some miles in the front of Silam, to give notice if a flotilla was seen advancing. Several of the native women and children went off to a house which had been hastily made for their reception in the depths of the forest behind the place, and W. put me into a small house on an adjacent hill, from whence, had the town been attacked, I and the women who remained with me could have been hastily hidden in the jungle, while a flanking fire could have been poured into any party attacking the fort.

Here I stayed for three or four nights, the rescued Bulungan men lying in a circle "heads and feet" with their weapons at hand, while I, Dato Gumbah's wife and others, slept in the centre.

The tentative state of affairs continued until at last we were gladdened by sighting in the far distance the smoke of a steamer. By and by the tops of the masts came into sight, and finally we made out that it was the old "Paknam" coming down to our assistance with supplies of men and ammunition.

These experiences occurred during the month of December 1885, and the "Paknam" being much overdue, our supplies were all exhausted, and our Christmas dinner that year consisted of plain boiled rice and boiled duck – no peas, no seasoning, no apple sauce, and worse than all no Christmas pudding, whilst our drinks consisted of Adam's ale, and tea in which we toasted our absent friends.

On another occasion, when going his rounds in the "Sabine," W. was informed that these same Omaddal people had again been committing various acts of piracy and murder, and that several persons captured by them were at a little village called Pakerangan; accordingly we went there. W. landed with a few police and seized the place, but the Bajows took the alarm on the launch's approach and fled into the forest at the back, taking with them two or three of the captured persons, including a woman whose husband they had murdered. The "Sabine" was anchored but a couple of hundred yards off the place, and I saw the Dyaks rush along a plank bridge into the chief's house, from whence wild yells and crashing sounds immediately proceeded, giving me the impression that a severe struggle was in progress. I watched with the greatest anxiety my husband balancing himself on the narrow pole leading to the house until he disappeared in it, but my fears proved groundless, as there was no one in the house except our own people, and it turned out that the Dyaks were simply celebrating the opportunity by shouting and smashing everything that came in their way and slashing at the kadjang walls, as there were no persons to attack. Seven men were recovered on this occasion.

Once when W. had to go down to punish the Bajows for committing another act of lawlessness, these same Omaddal people rushed across to the other side of the little island and getting into their boats, the men lay down in the bottom, the women poling them off, as they are 'cute enough when it suits their purpose, and were well aware that no order would be given to fire on them if their women were in danger.

In places where the Bajows have been brought under the direct influence of the Company's officials they are settling down very satisfactorily, building houses and becoming the main suppliers of firewood and attaps for thatching. They are even beginning to show a slight disposition to plant, and no doubt if an officer was permanently stationed in the Omaddal district a change for the better would be soon effected there. The absence of an official, on the other hand, is hardly fair to these people, as the only occasions when they come into contact with Western civilization is on one or other of these punitive expeditions; and no influence has yet been used to encourage them to adopt better habits.

Omaddal, owing to its position, the number of its inhabitants, and the amount of sea produce that exists in the seas round about, is one of the most important districts in the country, and would well repay attention.

Chapter IX.
Sulu and the Sulus.

Island of.—Bad characters.—Pugnacity.—Sea fight.—Pirates.—Cos-
tumes.—Handsome barongs.—Coast Sulus.—Agriculturists.—
Physique of.—Sulu Village.—Amenability.—Pioneers in Sulu.—Diff-
iculties of Sulu language.—Pearl diving.—Pearls.—Ponies.—
Viciousness of.—Spaniards.—Amuk.—Faithfulness of Amuk.—
Anecdote.—Jealousy.

Sulu is a small but very fertile and beautiful island situated in the Eastern seas about 24 hour's steam from Sandakan. It has been claimed by the Spaniards for some 250 years or thereabouts.[21] It may appear rather out of place to devote a chapter of this book to it, but the connection between it and Sandakan has always been very close, and the going and coming between the two places, has been and is very considerable, Sandakan drawing much of its supply of fruit, poultry, &c., from thence, besides which a large proportion of our population are Sulus.

The numerous islands constituting the Sulu group are of volcanic origin and very fertile. Sugh, as the Sulus call the main island, is a perfect gem of the sea, and together with Tapul and other islands, consists of open park-like glades, the trees for the most part being mango, durian, or other large fruit trees, or teak. The islands are small, the atmosphere is cool, a pleasant sea breeze is always blowing, and the inhabitants are very strong and healthy as well as numerous, and were it not for their combative nature which leads to constant acts of bloodshed, the population would rapidly increase and overflow. As it is, the war with the Spaniards which they ceaselessly wage is a continual drain, irrespective of the numerous village feuds which are always in progress. Yet notwithstanding this, these islands constitute the chief source of supply of immigrants to North Borneo.

Since the earliest records the Sulus have not borne a good name. Though not themselves actually pirates, communities of Illanuns and Balignini were always to be found haunting their neighbourhood, the Sultan and other headmen having the first pick, free of cost, of all persons captured by them in return for the shelter and encouragement they afforded these desperadoes. One of the consequences of this is, that the population is a very mixed one, Manilamen, Banjermassins, Singapore people, and others kidnapped by the pirates, forming no inconsiderable portion. Although the Sulus did not themselves practice piracy as a community, the more desperate and adventurous spirits amongst them frequently joined the pirates for a voyage or two, just for the fun of the thing, and would designate this as "jadi Balignini," but more frequently they acted as sailors on board the trading boats, which, heavily manned, used to pass to and fro between the numerous islands and the mainland. It was only owing to the existence of such a class of reckless and even ferocious sailors, prepared to fight at a moment's notice, that trade was able to be carried on at all in face of the chaotic state of affairs existing in these waters so recently as twelve years ago.

The innate love of combat was such, that they did not care who it was they fought so long as there was a fight. I remember the animation with which a young Sulu narrated an account of a sea-fight between Dato Beginda Putih and Dato Beginda Etam. The former (son of the well known pirate Dato Kurunding) having taken the seas, had already captured two or three trading prahus bound from Darvel Bay to Labuan, murdering every soul on board, when he came across his own cousin Dato Beginda Etam, and as when a pirate fleet is at sea it attacks every boat it meets regardless of ties of nationality or family, he at once went for his cousin, who fled, and a running fight ensued. Gelanee related with the keenest animation and delight the brave way in which the flags and banners flew; the deafening and defiant beatings of the gongs on both sides, as the long narrow boats bounded across a lively sea, their red, yellow and blue sails filled with the stiff breeze; the whoops and yells of both pursuers and pursued, (who quite entered into the spirit of the thing); the popping of the rifles, and the wild splashing as they frantically paddled through the dancing waters beneath a cloudless sky and a brilliant sun. The whole affair for those who love warfare and the sea must have been most exhilarating. There were some thirty boats in the engagement, but I did not gather which side Gelanee was on, this however was quite a detail.

The Sulus have a great love for brilliant colouring, and in their way, and according to their ideas, go in for very gay costumes. The cut of their clothes, though jaunty, is certainly not conducive to comfort, and in fact they sacrifice much to effect; the arms of their coats are so long and so tight that they fit like skins; and sometimes they are obliged to have their trowsers sewn on them or buttoned about the calves of their legs and ancles, so tight are they. Not only in the fit of their clothes are they great dandies but their garments are much decorated with embroidery, in which the Sulu women excel. It is no unusual thing to see trowsers of striped blue, magenta, and purple silk worn in conjunction with a coat of bright green satin, through which a gold pattern in stars is woven. A gay head-dress formed of a large square handkerchief much embroidered round the border is twisted about the head, one corner nattily screwed up over the left ear, with a very jaunty effect; round the waist a gay sash or cummerband, formed of two or three strips of brilliant coloured flannel sewn together, gives a finish to the costume. In the folds of the sash the sirih box is concealed, and also stuck through it is a handsome wooden sheath, which contains the broad and dangerous Sulu barong or sword without which no costume is complete.

The handles of their "barongs" are often very handsome, made of ivory, gold or silver, and beautifully chased, and in the case of ivory, skillfully carved. The buttons of their coats are often of gold or silver; they have a great love of jewellery and wear many rings, preferring those of very large size set with agates and cornelians or a greeny blue stone. The women often wear white bracelets and rings cut out of a sea shell which they call *galung tucyang*. They are not behind the men in their love and go in for many startling combinations.

When on the war path, the Sulu dandy shaves off one side of his moustache (if he boasts of such a facial decoration). This produces a very startling effect and is an intimation that he is ready to challenge the first comer.

The above remarks apply more particularly to the Coast Sulus: the "orang gimber" or agriculturists are not by any means such gay sparks, and furnish a class of much more reliable hard-working men. When threatened with oppression, however, they are found to be very stubborn, determined characters, though not so reckless as the "orang laut," nor do they love fighting for its own sake in the same way. The former class are very questionable additions to the population of a country, but the latter make a very useful and hard working community.

As regards their physique, the Sulus are rather above the ordinary Malay standard; they are very lithe, wiry and athletic rather than muscular, although there are exceptions, some of them being very strong and thick set.

On our estate, the Beatrice we have encouraged a great many Sulus to settle, preferring the "orang gimber." There is now quite a large and prosperous village of them all comfortably settled, the houses filled to overflowing, as new comers are constantly arriving to visit their friends. Many of these eventually settle down to a quiet agricultural life in a country where they are undisturbed and allowed to reap the fruits of their labours. From time to time, as occasion offers, we give them employment and find them on the whole, when fairly dealt with and not too hard pressed, a very satisfactory and reliable set of people, and quite law abiding.

The latter fact is all the more curious, as at home in Sulu they do not bear this character at all, and it serves to illustrate the force of habit and surroundings, as the same people we are told, when they return to Sulu, immediately assume a totally different attitude, and are most difficult to deal with.

The relationship existing between ourselves and them is of a feudal nature, the Sulus being expected to turn out and help in any way whenever occasion demands, they receiving for their labour their day's food and tobacco only. There is a sort of committee of head-men, who are responsible for the good behaviour of the whole body, and upon whose recommendation new comers are allowed to settle and enjoy the advantages along with the others. They are a happy, thriving and increasing body, and do well by the sale of their surplus bananas, pineapples, sugar cane, tapioca, and chickens.

The two following instances give an idea as to what sort of men the Sulus are when at home in Sulu. Pioneers there have an uncomfortable time, especially if they do not show consideration to the natives. The front door of a European home was quietly unhinged one night and laid on the lawn in front, where the inmates found it next morning; this was intended as a gentle hint that the people within were in the power of the natives, and must take greater care as to wounding their susceptibilities in the future or something more unpleasant would occur. On another occasion, some other Europeans, who had cut down fruit trees belonging to some Sulus, had a volley fired through their house over their heads as a warning.

The Sulu language is, in pronunciation, quite unlike Malay, being hard and gutteral, but when looked into, it is found that most of the words have their origin in Malay, though there are many which seem to point to a totally distinct root, but from whence these are derived I am unable to say. As for instance

water
Malay *ayer*
Sulu toobig
house
Malay *rumah*
Sulu bai
sea
Malay *laut*
Sulu dargat

I may mention here, that W. says the Sulu words signifying water, house, and sea, in Sulu, are in use in the Philippines also.

The Sulu Archipelago is chiefly famous for the pearls and pearl shells found in large beds in its shallow seas. The pearls are of great purity and value and occur in the large oyster, the same species as that found off the coast of Australia. Each individual shell is as large as a pie plate, and they are valued at about L40 per ton. The pearls are found in but few of them: the fishery operations being really carried on for the sake of the shells, and what pearls are obtained are regarded as prizes. Occasionally very large and fine ones are found, the largest I ever heard of was valued at $10,000, whilst the finest I myself ever saw was said to be worth $2,000, and was in size as large as the top joint of my thumb; it was however far from perfect, being neither good in shape or colour.

China is a great market for pearls, and a large proportion of those from the Sulu seas are sent there, as the prices the Chinese give are very high and they do not attach the same importance to shape and colour as we do.

There is no regular system of taxation in Sulu, but the Sultan reserves to himself the right of demanding as tribute all pearls above a certain size, when found, and there is a sort of myth extant, that the mother of the late Sultan has a measure, equal to a quart pot, full of them.

It is curious to see a poor-looking Chinaman take out of his pocket a little red rag, tied up into a parcel with a bit of string, and opening it display to one's view half a dozen pearls worth collectively several thousand dollars.

All Sulus are quite amphibious; some of them are remarkably good divers, and can descend to depths of 60 and 70 ft. without any apparatus or weight whatever, and bring up the oysters from the bottom.

As already mentioned, seed pearls are found in various places along our coast; these also command a price in China, where they are ground down to powder and used by the women, under the delusion that it will impart a pearly hue to their complexions.

The large grassy plains in Sulu, support a good many half-wild ponies, and it is from thence that we obtain our supplies. The Sulu ponies are small weedy vicious animals which act as if possessed by some evil spirit. They shy, bite, kick, and fight, and are altogether the most unreliable wicked little beasts ever invented. The only attempts yet made to put them between shafts, have ended in the speedy and entire destruction of the vehicle attached. One has been known to incapacitate three men in one afternoon, who all had to be borne to the hospital to be patched up.

The Sulu style of saddlery is primitive, the women ride astride as well as the men, and one make of saddle answers for both. The saddles proper are made of wood upon which a cushion is placed, the bridle is made of rope, a loop meeting at the back of the pony's neck, from which a single end extends, which is all that is grasped by the rider; a tuft of horse hair by way of ornamentation is placed over the front of the head halter, which should have the effect of making the animal squint.

Some fifteen years ago, the Spaniards determined to subjugate Sulu; the work has not advanced very far as yet, as, with the exception of the one walled city of Tiangai they have no foothold in the island; they dare not go outside its gates, and the walls are constantly patrolled by a cordon of sentinels. For some time after they occupied the place, the walls were of no great height, and were composed of palisades; it became a favourite amusement of the reckless Sulus to scramble over the barriers, rush through the town, cutting down every person they met, and then escape on the other side. On one of two occasions the town was nearly rushed altogether, and once at least the Spaniards closely missed being massacred. All this tended to cause the Sulus to regard the Spaniards with considerable scorn. Quite recently, a Spanish governor, reproving a young boy and striking him with his umbrella to give his words greater effect, was instantly cut down by the arrogant little imp.

The Sulus however have their good qualities, and they like and trust to those who are very true and staunch; Dato Haroun al Raschid came to Sandakan just before he was made Sultan of Sulu; the first time he had come here since his hostile visit in 1880. He went to pay his visit of ceremony to W. accompanied by a somewhat numerous retinue, all beautifully dressed and decorated, and fully armed also, as is customary. Just before he arrived however, we were somewhat astonished by the appearance of a still stronger body of Sulus, many of whom we knew personally. They waited about squatting in the verandah during the whole time the Dato was with us, and stopped after he had taken his farewell. When the Dato had gone we enquired the object of their visit, and after some time discovered it, for a Malay never comes direct to the point but always beats about the bush, and only discloses his real object just as he is leaving. It appeared they were aware of the Dato's intended visit, and knowing his ambitious nature, and former ill feeling, had come up to support us in case he should have tried any sudden coup. One of them told me they had a number of boats fully manned and armed close by, but hidden by fort Pryer ready for any emergency.

It was on this occasion, when conversing with the wife of one of the head-men, I enquired as to her ideas concerning polygamy. She said it did not put her about much. Her husband had once, taken a second wife but, she laughingly added "I stuck a knife in her, and soon got rid of her, and since then he has not tried it on any more."

Chapter X.
Malays.

Character.—Appearance.—Women's costume.—Religion.— Indolence.—Prodigality of nature.—Contentment.—Music.— Dancing.—Houses.—Property.—Language.—Domestic relations.—Divorce.—Kindness.—Children.—Massage.— Education.—Ornaments.—Polygamy.—Anecdote.—Marriage.— Needle work.—Sirih chewing.

A more charming or courteous race of people than the Malays, I have never come in contact with; from the highest to the lowest all are alike blessed with a charm of manner, that is very attractive; though deferential, there is not the faintest suspicion of servility about them, but they are perfectly easy and natural in manner. On visiting them, one is pleasantly received, conducted gracefully to the best place in the house, where a mat is spread to sit on, while the members of the household collect about, squatting upon the floor, and converse topics of local interest. Meanwhile orders have been given for chocolate which in due course is served with sweet biscuits, the mistress of the house doing the honours very prettily.

There is nothing boisterous, assertive, or rude in the Malay nature; in fact such characteristics are utterly lacking in their temperament, and there is about them nothing of the cringing servility of the Indian races. When once they know and respect anyone, the faith they repose is unbounded; they will come seeking advice, which given, is followed implicitly in the most childlike manner, and their devotion to those they love and trust, I have never seen equalled. In colour they vary from light to dark brown, the generality being of a coffee colour much like the Japanese. Many of the higher class women, and such as do not often leave their houses, are quite light in hue, resembling in complexion Southern Europeans. The type of face is Mongolian, the bridge of the nose almost flat, high cheek bones, and elongated eyes: the hair straight, luxuriant, and black; hands and feet small and delicately made.

They are personally very clean, bathing night and morning; and are very particular about washing their hands before eating, (which is the more necessary, as they eat with their fingers) neither do they omit to cleanse their mouths after every meal.

The women are very neat and spruce in their attire, which they change daily, their sarongs or skirts are often of very pretty patterns and colours, while their long loose kabyahs or jackets, which reach to their knees or below, are nicely made and finished off with a little edging. Their ornaments are brooches of a peculiar make, there being no catch to hold the pin, hair-pins, earrings, rings, and often bracelets. They affect no head coverings as a rule, but when they wish to be smarter then usual, throw large flowing veils of white or black net over their heads and decorate their hair with sweet smelling flowers and gold or silver pins. Although Mohammedans, they are never secluded, in Borneo at all events. They go barefooted, and dye their finger and toe nails with henna.

Were it not that they make their mouths so offensive by the disgusting habit they all indulge in of chewing sirih, they would be far more attractive-looking; as it is, their teeth are black and their mouths have the appearance of being full of blood. They have a strange way of filing their teeth across the front. The holes in the lobes of their ears are very large, often the size of a threepenny piece, and the style of earring much resembles a solitaire stud. If not possessed of earrings, they make little rolls of cloth, and stuff them through the holes, and sometimes push their cigarettes in them, for the women as well as the men smoke.

The Mohammedan religion, and the devout sentiments it instils into the hearts of the followers of the Prophet seems to me to be worthy at least of respect. I think a good deal of misunderstanding exists amongst Englishmen with regard to this faith. The root of the matter appears to be, that while the Jews had the Old Testament only, the Christians have the Old as well as the New Testament, and the Mahommedans have the Old, the New, and yet another new gospel in addition, which they contend supercedes the New Testament in the same manner as the New Testament with us supercedes the Old: it is not that they refuse belief in either the Old or the New Testaments any more than we Christians refuse belief in the Old Testament because we have received the New also.

There is no doubt of the sincerity of the Mohammedan, his open avowal of his faith quite puts to shame our pallid and deprecating treatment of religious matters in every day life. Wherever a Hadji may be at sundown, he then and there kneels down, his face to the setting sun, and says his prayers with clasped hands and upturned face, at intervals bowing his head to the ground.[22] It is a difficult, and indeed an almost impossible matter, to convert a Mohammedan to the Christian faith; the only chance is by working amongst the children whose ideas are not yet formed, and educating them up to our creed. Another instance of their steadfastness to their religious principles is their adherance to its precepts whatever they may be; they are the strictest teetotalers simply because forbidden by their religion to drink wine, and not because they have any dislike to it.

Much as I like the Malays, I must confess, however, they are not a hard working race. I fear their destiny is to disappear off the face of the earth at no very distant period, merged in the shoals of Chinese, Indians, *blacks* and others who are always turning their faces to this part of the world. It is not that they die out in the face of British civilization, for they thrive and do remarkably well under it, but that, not being a numerous race to commence with, and spread as they are over wide areas, they inter-marry with other Easterns and tend to form a mixed community in which their individuality is lost.

With regard to their laziness I am fain to suggest in their defence that, under like circumstances, even the go-a-head Anglo-Saxon race might degenerate and become as inert as they are. Nature is so lavish and so kind in her gifts in these favoured latitudes, that there is no incentive to labour; the smallest amount of work bestowed on the soil produces rich results, clothes are only needed for decency's sake, fuel only required for cooking and there is always more wood lying about than one knows what to do with, house-room is obtainable by the least amount of labour, and all the expensive tastes and habits which we are so rapidly augmenting in this nineteenth century, they know nothing about, and knowing nothing, have no desire or ambition to acquire wealth. Neither is there that keen struggle for existence, the incentive to labour, such as force the swarming Chinese to work from early morning to late at night for a bare pittance.

They carry their disregard for creature comforts in the matter of food to such an extent that it becomes the reverse of a virtue, in that they have one inducement, less to labour: they certainly do not live to eat but eat to live; anything as long as it staves off the cravings of hunger suffices for a meal, a few handfuls of plain boiled rice and a tiny bit of salt fish dried to a chip over a fire, satisfies them.

The Malays naturally are very musical, but their instruments are of a most primitive description, gongs and drums being the chief. A "Kalingtangan" is a series of small gongs of differing sizes placed in series on strings in a frame so that a scale of notes is obtained. The gongs are beaten with wooden hammers producing a very simple tune. This affords them great pleasure, however, and when once a mine-mine is started it goes on without intermission for three days and nights; the performers replacing one another at intervals. The sound carries a long way and is often plainly discernable two or three miles off, and is not disagreeable even to European ears. The drums are made of deer or snake skin stretched over a frame, the latter skin being the more valued for this purpose. Of European made musical instruments, so far as North Borneo is concerned, they give the preference to the concertina. They have concocted one tune of half a dozen bars which they play night and day; it is to be hoped for the sake of variety that they will soon learn or compose another. Some few aspire to the fiddle, but have not arrived at any particular tune. When paying visits to European houses the pianos are a source of great wonder, delight, and admiration, and they listen with the most rapt attention and pleasure to anyone performing, and are also greatly interested in the construction of these instruments.

Dancing of a sort, is an amusement of which they are fond, but it is chiefly the men who indulge in it. They make one or two shuffling steps to a species of waltz tune, but it is chiefly posturing they go in for, gay silk handkerchiefs being much in request, which they wave about in a light and airy fashion. The Sulu dances are entirely posturing; the performers scarcely move from one spot, but with outstretched arms twist and turn the fingers and move the hands; a little of this for an on-looker goes a long way, and after a couple of hours becomes even monotonous.

The houses are by preference built over the sea. The flooring is composed of lengths of split nebong (a kind of palm whose wood is very hard) placed at intervals, and through the interstices, which are numerous and wide, all the rubbish of the household is thrown into the sea below, so that when the tide rises it is carried away, and the space beneath the house left clean and tidy without the inhabitants having any trouble. Malay houses are not safe places to keep small articles in as they would quickly disappear like the household rubbish, but they are so barely furnished that there is hardly anything loseable through the floor. The open spaces are sometimes so numerous and large that it is positively alarming to walk about, while even in some of the best, it is almost equivalent to being educated for the tight rope to move in them; it is even possible to lie in bed and fish through the floor, and W. tells me that when first he arrived in Borneo and lived in a native house, he has actually done so. One portion of the house has a raised platform a couple of feet or so in height; this is set apart as the sleeping place of the married couple, and is surrounded by gaudy bed-curtains and surmounted by a canopy called a "lawang" also very brilliant in hue. In the day time the curtains are drawn up and reveal the contents of the platform, a mattress spread on the floor surmounted by a perfect mountain of pillows, behind which boxes are piled containing all the portable property of the family, pieces of T. cloth, chintz, silk sarongs, and clothing of all sorts; besides tea-cups, brass-trays, boxes, tea-kettles and such like articles. Otherwise there is no furniture whatever in the house, chairs and tables being unknown as the natives always sit tailor-fashion or squat on their heels; now and then one may come across a rough bench, but that marks a decided step towards civilization. Occasionally, if the house-owner is rich, several expensive gongs may be seen hung upon the walls, while there is always a creese or barong within reach.[23]

The Malay language is a soft and pretty one, easy to learn; one is not troubled by irregular verbs or any such intricacies as make European languages so difficult, yet it is almost as expressive.

No great affection exists between husbands and wives, but the mothers are always very much attached to their children. When a divorcee marries a new husband he is expected to provide for her whole family should she possess children, which he always does very cheerfully, and is as kind to the children as if they were his own. All natives in fact are very fond of, and good to children. Frequently stray children, known as "anak artim," are to be found in Malay villages belonging to nobody in particular, but taken care of by the community at large. It certainly does not cost much for clothing, as, until they are four or five years old, they wear little or no clothing beyond a necklace or bangles. The houses are so elastic that an odd two or three children can always find corners to curl up in, one finds them absolutely swarming with little naked brown creatures all very happy and dirty. The youngsters are prettily formed little things, very shapely and graceful, and resemble little animated bronze statues. Not Malay children only, but young Easterns of all countries are far less troublesome, noisy, and fractious than Europeans; they rarely cry or become a nuisance to any body. The babies even are comfortable, contented mites, and when able to toddle amuse themselves splashing and swimming about in the shallow seas, and rarely seem to get into real mischief or trouble.

Malay children are never carried in the arms as with us, but ride astride the mother's hip, she having to bend her body to accommodate the child, her arm being placed around it for support. Malay ideas with regard to the treatment of children are very elementary and incorrect, and it results in the survival of the fittest: they have not the faintest notion of medicine, or the cause of sickness, and consequently are quite unable to apply any remedy.[24] Whenever anybody is ill they always set it down to "demum" (heat or fever) or "anging tulong" (wind in the bones), however wide of the mark this diagnosis may be. They have some idea of massage, however, and frequently by this means relieve pain; I have often been afforded relief in this way when suffering from a stiff neck or slight rheumatism across the shoulders. A Malay woman kneads and manipulates one very gently and pleasantly, in fact all their actions are languerous, soft and graceful.

The mothers adopt very queer ways of arranging their children's hair; sometimes it is all shaved off, at another the head is entirely shaved with the exception of the top, where the hair is allowed to grow into a long straggling lock which falls over the unfortunate child's face and must be very teasing to the little one. In one instance I noticed the hair all shaved with the exception of two round spots, one on either side of the head which has a very comical effect.

According to their lights and knowledge, the Malays educate their children: the chief object is to teach them to repeat passages of the Koran by heart, and frequently through the thin walls of the houses one may hear all intoning together in a manner that a High Church curate would much envy.

The Malay women have great quantities of straight raven-black hair which they profusely anoint with cocoa-nut oil, and dress very neatly in a thick coil at the back of the head. They do not consider the toilet complete till they have stuck a series of gold or silver pins round the coil, or arranged a wreath of tiny sweet-smelling flowers around it, which is a very pretty fashion. Sometimes a small fringe of hair is cut and arranged across the forehead in European style.

A Mohammedan is allowed by his religion to have four true wives, but must never exceed that allowance: he may go in for the full complement at once if it so please him, and he feel competent to support so many at one time. As a rule Sulus have but one, while Malays often have two or three. In one family that I am well acquainted with, the husband has three. For a long time he had only one, but she went off her head, and after a few years he married another. Wife No. 1 was very peaceful, though vacant, a perfect cypher in the household after her calamity overtook her, poor woman, so No. 2 assumed the entire management of the home; but one fine day, to every body's intense astonishment, after a period nearly approaching seven years mental collapse, No. 1 woke up in full possession of her faculties. Then ensued an uncomfortable time for No. 2; squabbles, quarrels and jealousies of all kinds daily occurred, and the poor husband at last was driven to a third marriage for the sake of getting a little peace and comfort in his home.

Marriages are great opportunities for display, feasting, and merry making. A Malay girl is as much concerned about her bridal garments as an English belle. The ordeal is a somewhat long and trying one, for with a whitened face like that of a clown in a pantomime, she squats motionless, expressionless and silent, for hours at a stretch, beneath a gorgeous canopy, with curtains festooned and drawn aside so that she may be seen by the assembled company. A girl to support her on each side, performing in fact the duty of bridesmaids, while the gay throng circulate about the house laughing, chatting, smoking cigarettes, and chewing sirih, through all of which the bride has to preserve an impassive and stolid countenance. Everybody naturally wears their best clothes and the mingling of colours reminds one of a gay parterre. While in the back premises much preparing and cooking of comestibles is in progress.

The women, as I have mentioned elsewhere, are many of them very clever at embroidery, but the materials they employ are usually very inferior, which is a pity when one considers the hours devoted to the adornment of a single garment. They stretch the materials on a frame, before which they sit cross legged or squat on their heels, passing the needle up and down so regularly and beautifully that the back of their work is as good as the front, and it is difficult to tell which is which. The patterns are traced in the regulation way by pricking, and rubbing chalk through the holes. The designs in vogue are scrolls and conventional patterns, but not floral effects so far as I know. The silks in use are of Chinese manufacture, very fluffy and difficult to work with, but their clever fingers have a knack of twisting it slightly and making it work in very smoothly and evenly. Their combinations of colour leave something to be desired according to western notions of art, and the shades and colours obtainable are naturally somewhat restricted as well as crude in dye.

The Brunei women are great adepts at gold work, and embroider very elaborate mats and bolster ends in gold thread on scarlet cloth, which are very handsome and effective. They also weave bright coloured garments, sarongs more particularly, and have a mode of dying Chinese white silk in a series of large spots of varied colours which they greatly admire, and use it much for trowsers and handkerchiefs. The decoration on the coats is often very elaborate, applique designs sometimes being laid on with great effect. It is chiefly the men's clothes that are ornamented with embroidery &c., the wives of the household vieing with each other in the production of gay coats and turbans for the adornment of their lord and master.

Every Malay carries a sirih box, without which his toilette would not be complete; just as in the old days our great grandfathers and grandmothers carried their snuff boxes; both habits I consider repulsive, and do not see much to choose between them. Women as well as men are addicted to this horrid habit. The sirih boxes are usually made of brass, prettily chased, but now and then silver boxes are used. They contain three or four tiny receptacles, also of brass, for the lime, etc., and a pair of betel-nut cutters, and a tiny spoon with which to spread the lime on the sirih leaf. Fresh sirih leaves, small bits of betel (or areca) nut, resembling fragments of nutmeg, lime made from burned and pounded sea shells, and a cube or two of gambier are the necessary ingredients; a small atom of each wrapped up in the leaf affords much enjoyment. It is also said that sirih chewing allays thirst and sustains persons when travelling, about this I cannot speak personally for I have never been able to get up sufficient courage to try.

Plate 7 T. Ficken, 'View from Near the Rahjah's Cottage', lithograph, from Spenser St John, *Life in the Forests of the Far East: Travels in Sabah and Sarawak in the 1860s*, London, 1873. *Source:* National Library of Australia, Canberra.

CHAPTER XI.
SINGAPORE TO SANDAKAN.

The voyage from England to Singapore has been so often related that a
description of the four weeks spent upon a P.&O. steamer would be but
wearisome repetition, so I will pass over that part of the journey and begin
this paper with an account dating from Singapore.[25]

I have not been a great traveller, consequently my experience is not very
extensive, but in the course of my wanderings I have never visited a more
delightful place than Singapore, and the opportunity of describing it I
cannot resist. The scenery at the westward entrance to the Harbour is very
lovely, narrow straits dotted with islands, some large, some smaller, but
all clothed with luxuriant foliage to the water's edge, while a brilliant sun
sheds a glamour over the scene, the rippling water reflects the blue
heavens above, and the white sails of little boats skimming to and fro,
complete as delightful a picture as can be desired.

The Docks at Singapore are situated a long way from the town. The
drive to the European quarter through the native portions of the
settlement is a very uninteresting one, for the way lies through newly
reclaimed land and a wilderness of bricks and mortar, cuttings into stiff
clay hills, half built houses etc.; no trees line the way and the sun pours
down on dusty roads with overwhelming strength. I think that many
travellers who are merely passing through with only a limited time at their
disposal, do not gain a fair idea of the beauties of the place, their
explorations rarely extending beyond a drive to the town, a tiffin at an
hotel, a few purchases from Bombay or Chinese stores, and the return
drive along that same hot, dusty and tiring road to Tanjong Paggar
Wharf, or beyond, wherever their steamer may lie.

Singapore as I know it is a perfect paradise, full of shady avenues of
flowering trees, waving palms, great leaved bananas and huge clumps of
feathery bamboos, through whose thin leaves the winds murmur a soft
rustling song all day long, smooth velvety lawns, well kept gardens in
whose centres lie the great cool houses surrounded by broad shady

verandahs; even the hedges are made of the gorgeous scarlet-flowered hibiscus, and the lovely yellow alamanda with its large glossy leaves grows in great clumps, adding with the bourgain-villea, flamboyant and scarlet flowered tulip tree, touches of welcome colour amongst the profuse and luxuriant masses of greenery.

As for the roads they are superb, leaving nothing to be desired. Even in England I have seen none better kept, while as to the East they are unrivalled. Great channels on either side carry off the heavy rainfall, avenues of trees shade them from the hot sun; and driving in the early morning or cool evening is very interesting and enjoyable, added to which all the objects that meet the eye are totally unlike those at home. One after another are to be seen Indian coolies carrying bundles of long grass for their ponies to eat, carts full of pine apples, unwieldy buffaloes, two prosperous looking celestials seated side by side in a Victoria driven by a Malay syce, and drawn by a pair of very fine horses, a row of Chinamen squatting upon their heels on the top of a low wall.[26] Then a market is passed by, full of mal-odorous jack fruit, lying side by side with delicious mangosteens, luscious pines or refreshing oranges.

Next is seen a chetty (Hindoo banker) clad in an elongated bath towel with a dab of whitewash on his forehead, then a gang of shiney black spindle-shanked Kling roadmakers lightly attired in bathing drawers and big turbans.

The conveyances chiefly affected by the lower classes in Singapore are jinrickshas, a sort of perambalator with shafts like miniature hansome cabs drawn by Chinese coolies, usually very lean but with an enormous development of the muscles of their calves. It is wonderful to remark the strength with which a man, a perfect bag of bones, drags along the ricksha in which are seated, pleasantly conversing or fanning themselves, two big fat men of his own nationality who regard their unfortunate countryman merely as a beast of burden, and worthy of no more pity or sympathy than a dog or mule. These rickshas are only used by the Chinese and natives: Europeans and half castes, as well as wealthier Chinamen affect hack carriages called gharries, vehicles not unlike our growlers, drawn by fiery little Battick ponies. These tiny animals are perfect wonders of strength in their way, pretty little creatures scarcely bigger than shetland ponies, with flowing tails and manes, fiery restless eyes and dilating nostrils, dashing along at reckless speed in the most undaunted manner, although they may have a load of five persons besides the carriage behind them.

The European residents drive victorias, landaus and buggies drawn by fine Australian horses. The Singaporeans pride themselves on their knowledge of horse flesh and are very fond or racing.

One of the show places is Whompoa's garden. Whompoa, as his name denotes, was a Chinaman and the tale I was told about him, is that in his early days he was employed in a Hongkong bakery at a time when China was at war with England. Certain mandarins conceived the idea of ridding themselves of the entire English garrison and everyone else in Hongkong at one bold stroke, and to this end they incited the bakers to mix arsenic in the bread. Whompoa, one of the men, having a partiality for the English informed the British officers. This information arrived almost too late, for the bread had already been delivered. Warning was at once sent round and in nearly all cases the mischief was prevented, nevertheless several persons were very ill, and one or two I believe died. The authorities being fully alive to the fate which would have overtaken Whompoa had he remained in Hongkong, sent him to Singapore and set him up in business there. He throve and prospered and finally became very wealthy and much respected. Such is the tale as it was told to me.

The garden covers a large extent of ground and is full of curious and interesting trees, shrubs and flowers as well as several animals. There are also large tanks in which flourish the magnificent Victoria Regia lily. Trees cut and trimmed into the shapes of grotesque animals and birds stand at most of the corners of the paths, and here, as elsewhere in Singapore, elk horn ferns hang pendant in great masses from the branches of the higher trees.

A curious feature which strikes a new comer and will probably keep him, if staying in the country or suburbs, awake the first night, is the ceaseless whirring and buzzing sounds made by myriads of insects and other creatures of all kinds, which commence at sun down and do not cease until morning. Cicadae, mole crickets, night grasshoppers, distant frogs and goat suckers, besides many others go to make up the chorus, the result being a soft ceaseless murmuring sound, very soothing and pleasant when once one is accustomed to it.

When staying in Singapore it is not uninteresting to visit an animal collector's premises, there are usually two or three such establishments to be found hidden away in the native town. At such a place you may find newly trapped and very savage tigers in very small and apparently insecure cages, baby orangutans, small elephants, monkeys by the dozen, parrots, mynahs, argus and fire-back pheasants, peacocks, apes, &c., and sometimes a real curiosity such as a black leopard, a tapir or rhinoceros, all waiting for shipment to distant Zoos.

One point which strikes the observer is the absence of squalid and grimy poverty such as is so apparent in England.[27] The people may be, and no doubt often are, poor enough, but their wants are few and easily supplied and hunger is virtually unknown. Clothes are merely required for decency's sake, and with such bright genial surroundings, their spirits are more buoyant than would be possible in this cold grey England of ours; in a word, brightness, colour and prosperity seem to me the chief attributes of this thriving and delightful little colony. The brilliance of the sun reflected in the sparkling water of the harbour, the greens of the trees, the lovely flowers which grow in such profusion, the waving palms, the clumps of feathery bamboos through whose rustling leaves the soft winds sigh, the velvet-like laurels which never grow parched or dry, the fine red roads, the cosmopolitan crowds which throng the busy streets, the strange chatter of a babel of unknown tongues and the unaccustomed sights which meet the eye at every turn, are full of fascination to the uninitiated and for me they have a never failing charm.

The meaning of Singapore is, Singa to call, and Pura a city, or otherwise port of call, a name it justly deserves, for the number of ships which look in there is very considerable, lying on the high road between Europe and India on the one side and China on the other, while it is the centre of a large transhipment trade between Batavia, Sumatra, Borneo, North and South, Australia, Bangkok, Malacca, Macassar, all the Native States, the Eastern and Australian Islands generally, and Saigon, China and Japan beyond.[28] It is the second biggest coaling port in the world and probably the largest distributor of rice, which brought from Siam and neighbouring parts by thousands of tons, is sent off by the local boats to the islands eastwards which do not raise sufficient for their own consumption. Important though Singapore is, it is only yet in the infancy of its prosperity compared with what it will be in the future when the Native States and the Islands of the Eastern Seas are further developed than at present. As to the number of ships that call there now, I remember on one occasion when looking out for the arrival of a relative from England, that no less than seventeen vessels were signalled at the signal station on Fort Canning as coming in through the westward passage alone, between the hours of six and seven o'clock one morning, besides several from the eastwards.

A curious odour of its own pervades Singapore, not by any means unpleasant, and mainly suggestive of spices, pineapples and flowers. It is sometimes plainly discernible when the steamer is still some miles out at sea if the wind is blowing off the land, but is not so perceptible when you are once there.

A drive across the whole breadth of the little island to Changie the police station opposite to the mainland of Johore is very interesting. The way lies past cocoanut groves, indigo fields, lemon-grass estates, tapioca plantations and other un-English cultivations, with here and there a jungle covered hill in which often lurk tigers. The road all the way is excellent wide, hard, red, and kept in splendid condition, flanked on either side by deep dykes to carry off the heavy rain-fall, while most of the way it is sheltered from the ardent sun's rays by avenues of flamboyant trees whose gorgeous scarlet blossoms in conjunction with the full green of these trees is very pleasing to the eye.

The town of Johore as regarded from Changie, is extremely pretty, every height is crowned with a handsome building in the centre of a fine garden.[29] The Sultan's palace occupies the right foreground, while Mosques, schools and other public buildings, besides the private residences of Europeans embosomed amongst rich tropical foliage, are scattered across a frontage of some two miles. The Strait itself is about ⅓ of a mile across. I may take this opportunity of tendering my thanks to the Sultan for his many acts of thoughtful kindness in placing at our disposal steam launches and other facilities, for getting about whenever we have visited Johore.

The return drive to Singapore, if made towards nightfall, gains an additional interest from the fact that tigers are nearly always known to frequent some parts of the way; I have often had my heart in my mouth when turning a bend in the road near to which there may be a remnant of jungle left, but although the tigers are undoubtedly, not far off, yet they have never been known to attack a carriage, and are mean-spirited beasts, never making a bold front attack. In 1883 when W. was crossing the island, a tiger was caught in a pig pit within 100 yards of the road, and was lying at the bottom of it when he passed.

The hospitality always shown by the Singaporeans to new comers or passers through accredited with letters of introduction is a very pleasant feature in a visit to this delightful place, making the break in the voyage particularly enjoyable; the large spacious houses, the great cool verandahs, and big airy rooms being no small luxury after the confinement and heat inseparable from ship-life, added to which the genial welcome is a charming contrast to the chilly insular reserve one is accustomed to at home.

I am told that I have been very fortunate in having cool weather on my several stays in Singapore, still I could have wished it two or three degrees cooler.

In addition to the number of steamers alongside the extensive wharves, many more lie anchored in the road opposite the town, men of war of all flags and merchantmen lending much interest and variety to the scene as viewed from the Esplanade, while numerous boats and lighters, here called sampans and toongkongs ply between the shore and the ships carrying passengers and cargo. The change from the fine comfortable P. and O. steamer to the little local boat in which the remainder of the voyage to Borneo has to be undertaken, is very great and cannot be accounted an agreeable one, especially when crowded by coolies as they sometimes are. Most of them boast of a particularly fine and large description of cockroach, a most loathsome beast. Coolies sometimes occupy every available inch of the deck, and what between them above and cockroaches below, the life of a first class passenger is not a very enjoyable one, though I freely and gratefully acknowledge that the captains do all in their power, even to the lending of their own deck cabins, to alleviate the discomforts one has to put up with. There are cabins in the saloon but they are rarely used except as dressing rooms, being far too hot and confined, not to speak of the aforesaid cockroaches and rats, to allow of sleeping in, so, when night time comes, the China boys may be seen wandering about with mattresses and bedding, making little camps at different points of vantage on deck, such as the skylight which is always a favourite refuge, the top of the hatch if big enough etc. When one has retired to rest, one's slumbers may probably be broken by the incessant chatter of a group of Sikhs, in charge perhaps, of a batch of prisoners; after a time one gets impatient and cries "Diam," be quiet, whereupon a more considerate Malay prisoner (who may perhaps be charged with murder) suggests to his guard that the "mem" (lady) wants to go to sleep. It is a very public state of existence this, Malay women with their babies, Chinese coolies, Dyak gutta hunters, Arab traders, ponies, cattle, pigs, chickens, ducks, all crowd the deck in the most chaotic confusion, yet all seem happy, and most good naturedly make the best of the circumstances.[30] The men squeeze themselves as small as they can when one is treading over their prostrate bodies, and the mothers sweep their numerous progeny out of the way, and I must say that they are far less objectionable than a similar crowd of low class English would be under like circumstances. They all take a very kindly interest in me, and I remember on one occasion how an Arab trader commiserating my sufferings from sea-sickness, undertook to cure me with a decoction of pepper and lemon juice, but the poor man's good intentions were of no avail as I found the remedy much worse than the disease.

The passage money, notwithstanding all these discomforts, is proportionately much higher than that of the P. and O. or Messagerie lines, the fact being that competition so far as passenger steamers is concerned has not set in. The time required to accomplish the journey between Singapore and Sandakan varies from five to seven days, according to the length of stay made at the different ports on the way. It takes from three to three and a half days to steam from Singapore to Labuan, during which time one sights no land except the group of islands known as the Natunas, and steamers are rarely met with.

Labuan is a small island off the main island of Borneo, and it is the smallest of British colonies. In days gone by, it was a far more populous place than at present, though latterly it has been coming to the fore again, and will no doubt in time become of more importance than it is at the moment, as it possesses coal of good quality and unlimited quantity, while the trade of the several rivers of importance opening on to Labuan Bay, will in time, as population grows, cause it to become a considerable depot and centre.[31]

The grounds attached to Government House at Labuan are charming, and quite park like in their effect and the house itself is a big rambling but very convenient building. Labuan boasts of many orchards and gardens, and from it, and the island of Sulu, North Borneo has hitherto chiefly drawn its supplies of fruit. Here are to be seen plantations of cocoanuts, orange, lime, and mangosteen, besides durian, langsat, rambutan, banana, and most other tropical fruits. The Labuan mango has been brought to great perfection, chiefly owing to the attention bestowed upon it by Sir Hugh Low, when Governor of the colony.[32] Most of these fruits take from 7 to 10 years to come into bearing, mangosteens even longer, and as North Borneo only dates back a few years, and other more pressing matters had to be attended to before planting was taken in hand, there has hardly yet been time for the fruit trees here to come to maturity.

Having left Labuan, the rest of the voyage is accomplished by skirting the coast line; the next call is at Gaya which is the first of the B.N.B. Company's ports, and boasts of grand and majestic scenery. From here one gets a view of Kina Balu the largest mountain in all Borneo, nearly 14,000 feet high, a fine and cloud-capped object in the landscape, far out-topping its compeers, though some of them are of no mean height. The stay at Gaya does not extend beyond a few hours, barely allowing time for the shipment of some native cattle, pigs, etc., and then a hurried departure is made to save day light, for the entrance to the station is dangerous and cannot be accomplished after dark. Delay means money lost to the owners of the ship.

Some twelve hours or so later Kudat is reached, the centre of distribution of supplies for the Maludu Bay Tobacco Estates. The sunsets at these northern ports are wonders of colour and beauty, so clear, vivid and intense are the lights and shadows. The rays of the setting sun reflect their beauties on the rippling waters of the Bay, while the land beyond and around deepens in hues of blues and purples, and the coral shallows shine forth in vivid tender greens. A stillness reigns supreme, broken only by the incessant chatter of gathering flocks of birds, collecting in the feathery top of a tall palm tree, their usual roosting place.

Only a short stay is made here, and once again the anchor is weighed, the order for departure given and we are off on our way once more. About this part of the voyage the day's monotony is not unfrequently broken by the capture of fish. The mode of fishing is somewhat odd; a long line is procured with a large strong hook at the end, the bait consisting of a piece of white rag, in-board a bight is taken in the line and tied by a piece of twine, and a bell is attached to this part. When a fish, springing at the white rag is hooked, it breaks the twine causing the bell to ring, upon which there is a general rush of every body to the spot, it frequently needing the combined efforts of three or four men to haul in the capture, while everyone waits in anxious suspense to see the result. Sometimes the fish overjumps the hook and escapes, but usually he is safely landed, generally a fine "alo-alo," a large pike-like fish of up to 60 lbs. in weight, which affords a welcome change to our dinner-table, as well as that of the crew and many other passengers, as they are very good eating.

CHAPTER XII.
SANDAKAN.

Sandakan Bay.—Bahalla heads.—The town.—Steam launches.—
Fort Pryer.—Government offices.—Fish market.—Population.—
Revenue.—Farms.—Laws.—Slavery.—Constabulary.—Roman
Catholic schools.—Health.—Temperature.—Seasons.—Rain.—
Length of day.—Elopura.

Sandakan is situated on the N.E. coast of Borneo just within the bay whose name it bears. It is distant about seven days steam from Singapore, while from Hongkong it is four and a half to five days. The communication with Singapore is most irregular although there are four steamers on the run, two of which proceed to the eastward as far as the Moluccas. The connection with Hongkong is more to be depended on, one steamer being regularly employed to run between Borneo and that little but most important and thriving colony to the north of us. Telegraphic communication there is none, so that we are wholly dependent on the steamers for news. It will therefore be understood with what interest we look for their arrival, and our impatience when we get no mails for three or four weeks.

Sandakan Bay is a very fine natural harbour. The entrance is one and a half miles broad. Inside the headlands it increases to seven miles in breadth, while its length is about twenty miles: about seventeen more or less navigable rivers flow into it. The entrance is guarded by the grand and defensive sandstone cliffs of Bahalla, whose precipitous faces softly toned to all the varying shades of reds and purples, face the eastern sky, while at their feet luxuriant foliage flourishes, and little palm-leaf houses peep out from amidst the greenery and dot the gleaming white shore. A fort erected on the top of Bahalla would make Sandakan perfectly secure from the attack of any enemy, while the splendid landmark the bold cliffs afford, enable Captains of vessels to steam safely into port at any hour of the day or night without a pilot.

After rounding Bahalla you will soon find yourself opposite the town, which, lying on the north side of the bay, is concealed from sight until you are along side it. It has a frontage of over two miles, but no depth, steep hills springing up but a short distance from the shore, except in one part where there is a gradual rise inland; as a comparison I may mention that it much resembles Dover. These hills are capped by houses, the homes of the European residents, and at night when the lamps are lit in the bungalows, the effect is a bright and pretty one as viewed from the sea.

The business portion of the town lies at the foot of these hills, a considerable number of the streets being built over the sea, on piles made of iron-wood or brick, and raised jetties for foot passengers, answering the purposes of roads and side walks run along the front of them. There are no wheeled vehicles of any kind allowed in Sandakan, even the despised ricksha being interdicted! while it will be understood that they are hardly suited even for ponies to pass along. All the conveyance of baggage, rice, stores &c., &c. is done by carry-coolies who bear the loads slung on ropes, suspended by poles from shoulder to shoulder. The shops themselves are made of either wood or brick according to the means of the owner. There is not much uniformity about them; some are tall, some are squat, some are painted a bright yellow while others are green or red, and others again boast of no paint at all; there is a delightful irregularity about them, every man being his own architect and house decorator, so that the effect is bizarre in the extreme.

The Government jetty is some 600 feet long with a T head. At the end is a coal godown and a store, while half way down the length of the wharf is the Custom House flanked by its barricade.[33] Within the over-lapping heads of the pier lie the steam launches belonging to the various estates, smart little crafts ready to steam off with the great lighters in tow, carrying to the estates on the rivers live stock, doors and windows, cases of Pilsener beer, bags of rice and salt fish, and attaps for house thatching, while perched upon the top of all this heterogeneous cargo are seated the newly arrived coolies with their modest baggage.

The chief object to the right, as viewed from the sea, is Fort Pryer, from which floats the B.N.B. Co's flag. It is a small round natural hill occupied by the police, thoroughly commanding the town, so that in the case of a riot the Constabulary would have every advantage. There are several guns there which however have only so far been needed for saluting purposes. To the right of the fort and immediately behind it are the barracks and gaol, all dominated over by the Commandant's house which is perched on a hill above.

The Government offices are situated in the centre of the town, not far from which are two large well built brick hotels, while the new Club House, a less pretentious, but solid wood building, is fast nearing completion. These buildings all look upon the Lawn Tennis ground. Government House lies to the left of the town on a slight eminence, but hidden from view by clumps of bamboo and African oil palms. Beyond again, and further along the shore, are two large Saw Mills. In a convenient position, with a garden surrounding it, is the hospital and dispensary with coolie wards in the rear.

The town proper is mainly composed of traders' shops, built over the water, for the convenience of the native traders who are thus able to bring their boats, containing jungle and sea produce to the foot of the ladders communicating with the houses. Roads, bridges, barracks, gaol, offices, government quarters, the town lighting by means of kerosene lamps, are looked after by the P.W.D.[34]

The fish market is quite a feature of the place, and is daily supplied with a fine and varied assortment of fish, from prawns to rock cod. Situated as it is over the water it is easily kept clean. Here and in the neighbouring shops there is a sort of bazaar, in which are sold fruit, vegetables, salt fish, cakes and other commodities. The one trade of sirih leaf selling, alone employs a good many persons.

The places of worship are many and various, there is an Anglican Church with a well attended school for boys, while the establishment of the Roman Catholics is but a few hundred yards distant. Here again is a flourishing boys' school, while at the Convent, the five sisters are doing good work in educating little girls and rescuing tiny deserted babies. A substantial Joss House, where the Chinese worship, is closer to the town, while behind the Government offices is situated the Mosque to which the Mohammedans flock on Fridays, while close to the barracks is a Sikh temple.

The population is a very cosmopolitan one composed of British, Germans, Dutch, Malays which includes Singapore and Penang men, Bruneis, Dyaks, Bajows, Sulus, Bugis, Banjermassins, Javanese, Chinese, Sikhs, Indians, Arabs, Somalis, &c. The total population as shown by the last census was over 6,000 persons, of whom 129 were Europeans, a very considerable number being ladies and children. When first I came to Sandakan there was only one other English woman in the place.[35]

The chief source of revenue, leaving land sales out of the question, is derived from what are termed "farms;" that is, the letting of the sole monopoly of dealing in any particular commodity out to certain persons or firms such as the Spirit farm, the Opium farm, the Gambling farm, and the Pawnbroking farm.[36] Except for spirits, opium and tobacco, Sandakan is a free port. Export of jungle produce and such like have to pay a royalty of 10 per cent; this is in lieu of the persons who collect, having to pay for licences.

The laws in force in the territory are taken from the best and most suitable sources, and include the Indian Civil and Penal Codes. A Mohammedan priest, known as an Imaum appointed and paid by Government, dispenses justice amongst the Mohammedans, and presides over a divorce court, as it is necessary that he should regulate all matters of a domestic nature amongst followers of the Prophet. His time is a good deal taken up in Court, as these people seem to pass most of their spare time in marrying and giving in marriage, and then getting divorced, after which they usually start again on the same round.

A European police court magistrate always sits, and Sessions Courts are held from time to time as required. Appeals from the lower Courts are taken by the Governor in the Supreme Court. Sentences of death in the Sessions Court have to be confirmed by the Governor, who issues the death warrant.

The Land laws provide for a certain amount of work being done on all land sold, or else after a specified lapse of time the grants are confiscated.

In accordance with the terms of the Royal Charter, slavery is not yet entirely abolished, but measures have been taken to modify it, and its ultimate extinction is a mere matter of time. All children born of slave parents since 1883 are free, while the importation of any fresh slaves is prohibited, neither are slaves allowed to be bought or sold in the territory.

The Constabulary force of some 300 men officered by Europeans, is mainly composed of Sikhs and Dyaks, who have to undertake the duties either of policemen or regular soldiers as occasion demands.

The Roman Catholic Establishment under the guidance of Father Byron is doing much good work in a quiet unobtrusive way amongst the children (Chinese, Japanese and Malay). Father Byron knowing well that it is almost an impossibility to convert adult Mohammedans or Chinese, wisely devotes himself to the education of such children as he can get to attend his school, while the Mother and Sisters ably assist the good work forward by instructing the little girls, and caring for the small babies.

The health of Sandakan is very good; as a testimony to this, I may mention that nearly all the members of the government staff in 1882 are still here, and absences from office on account of ill health are very rare. If there are any cases of sickness they are usually to be attributed to carelessness, or inattention on the part of the sufferer, such for instance, as turning over the soil below or near the house, standing about in wet clothes in an airy verandah after violent exercise, or taking quinine when suffering from a slight touch of sun, under the mistaken idea that it is fever: or some other such infringement of common sense laws.

The temperature rarely rises above 86° in the houses, or falls below 72°. We always need a covering over us at night, and although we had a punkah above our dining table, for three years I never once saw it in motion.[37] This is a significant fact when one considers that we are situated in latitude 5. N. Although it is extremely hot in the afternoon, we are never driven to the expedients for cooling the air, such as they have to adopt in houses in India and China in the hot season, and all the doors and windows are thrown open to let in the breeze instead of being closely shut to keep out the heat as in those countries.

The differences in the seasons are not strongly marked. At Christmas and New Year time we usually have a greater rainfall than at any other, we also get a second sub rainy spell about June, the rest of the year the rain-fall is fairly evenly distributed. We get four to five times as much rain in one year as falls in England in the same period of time. The rain certainly does not descend in a half hearted manner but in a perfect deluge. It is very curious and interesting to hear the rain storms advance; first you are dimly conscious of a soft rushing sound afar off, this augments and approaches minute by minute, then the leaves on the surrounding trees begin to rustle, the sound increases and comes nearer, squalls of wind shake the house causing a frantic scurry to shut up all doors and windows, a few premonitory drops patter on the ground, and then with a sudden roar, torrents of blinding, sweeping rain are upon you.

Being so near the equator there is very little difference in the length of the day at either solstice. In June the sun rises at ten minutes to six and sets at ten minutes past. In December it rises at ten minutes past six and sets at ten minutes to, there thus being a total variation in the course of six months of forty minutes in the days' length. It is customary to say that there is no twilight in tropical countries but this is not quite correct, as in June there is a perceptible difference in the length of the day, in addition to the twenty minutes above referred to.

Elopura, the name originally given by W. to the new town, has been superseded by that of Sandakan (the name of the old settlement), which has led to considerable confusion, as the original name yet appears on most maps and several title deeds and documents.

The houses we live in may be roughly described as big airy barns, built above ground on poles, with thatched roofs and palm leaf walls. There is a certain kind of novelty suggestive of a perpetual pic-nic about life in them, and when I first arrived it appeared to me rather unwise opening my baggage, and storing my belongings in such a fragile and airy tenement, as though one was asked to take up one's permanent abode in a summer house – indeed, even summer houses at home are more substantially built and shut in than are our domiciles. A large open umbrella might perhaps be a better comparison. For coolness and suitability however they are not to be excelled, and being all on one floor there is no tiresome running up and down stairs.

They are surrounded by broad verandahs, most delightful lounging places, liberally furnished with long bamboo chairs and ornamented with trophies of the chase, such as deer and buffalo horns, and rendered more attractive still by stands of flowers, foliage plants and lovely ferns. It is customary to take early coffee and afternoon tea in the verandah, and it is also a cool resort after dinner.

The house, or bungalow properly speaking, is usually situated in the centre of a flower garden, which is always more or less open, while to the house itself there is also no entrance door, so that any one can walk up into the verandah.

The garden is bright and gay all the year round with many kinds of handsome flowers, hibiscus of four or five different kinds, double and single, from full red to creamy white, and also the fuchsia variety, alamandas, oleanders, bourgainvilleas, gardenias, roses, jassmines of two or three sorts, honey suckle, lillies red and white, begonias, chlorodendrons of three species, passion flowers, Honululu creeper and many others whose names I do not know, all flourish and bloom to perfection in the open air, and need but little care.

The servants are usually Chinese, and if Chinese, generally Hainans, people coming from the island of that name not very far from Hongkong. Our servants are Cantonese, I prefer them to the Hainans, as they are smarter in appearance, and tidier than the latter. The Chinese are a most conservative race and very cliquey; I have often been amused to hear a boy talking the most infamous and incomprehensible Malay to a fellow countryman, and have said "Boy, what for you talkee Malay along that Chinaman" to which the reply is a scornful "He no belong true Chinaman, he belong Shanghai man, he no can savee my talkee.'[38]

Our boy and cook we have had for many years, and very good servants they are. The cook has a very suggestive name for a man of his profession, – Lam Chong, – who more usually goes by his sobriquet of "Lamb Chops," he is a most honest fellow of a lugubrious cast of countenance, but he always rises to the occasion, and the greater the difficulties he has to encounter, the more cheerful he becomes. He has accompanied us on many an up country journey and behaved most loyally, surmounting all obstacles. When making these long journeys up rivers to the far interior, he has provided us with our meals quite regularly, and prepared as well, and in almost as great variety as though we had been at home, yet the only fire he had, was a very primitive arrangement; a clay fire-basket made in a turned up box filled with sand.

His sole duty is to provide our meals and to do the necessary marketing; to this end he every morning makes an early journey to the town, a basket on his arm and an umbrella in his hand. At the market he buys meat, fish, vegetables, bread, etc. sufficient for the day's consumption. Lam Chong is a most conscientious account keeper: he and I frequently have differences of opinion as to the total of the score, and the matter has to be held over for W.'s arbitration when he is usually found to be correct. At first I did not understand his strange and gloomy manner of coming back after five minutes absence, and placing 20 cents by my side declaring in a positive manner that the account "no belong ploper."

Some persons prefer contracting with their cooks to cater for them at so much a day; during the last three years the charge per day has risen from $1.00 to $1.50 per head, which shows how the price of provisions has gone up. Servants' wages have also risen in a proportionate degree. The reason of this upward tendency is the inadequacy of the local supplies. Fresh market gardens, piggeries, poultry yards, and fruit and vegetable patches are constantly being opened in the suburbs, and this matter will no doubt work its own cure in course of time, at any rate it is to be hoped so. The extreme cost of provisions however is largely due to the high prices at which the restricted number of Market stalls are sold month by month at auction.

Lam Chong belongs to a Dinner giving Club. Sometimes after these festivities soup is about ten minutes late and when it is served is very bad, after which a long wait ensues before fish arrives, about this period Lam Chong's voice in loud declamation is heard from the cook-house: a conjunction of these three circumstances always leads us to guess that it has been one of his Dinner Club evenings. Occasionally he gets very bad indeed, throws himself on his bed, tears down his mosquito curtain, smashes the bed posts and involves all his surroundings in one general chaos. This does not happen often, however, and we have to put up with his occasional eccentricities on account of his general good conduct and faithfulness, and as he once with the aid of our Doctor, by his nursing largely contributed towards pulling my husband through a nearly fatal illness, my partiality for him will be understood.

Once Lam Chong was sent for by his mother, who had nominated a wife for him, and considered it high time for him to lay aside his bachelorhood. Lam Chong begged leave of absence, which granted (he having previously provided us with a man to act as his substitute during his absence) he obediently set sail for China and disappeared into space, and I thought I had lost him for ever. The new cook did not answer at all – and for three months I was driven from pillar to post by a succession of incapables, until at last in despair I sent general messages up to China,

---

*   Poor Lam Chong, since the above was penned, has joined the great majority; through his death we have lost a very faithful servant.

that Lam Chong must come back. I had not the faintest idea where he was, but sure enough by the next steamer two or three persons brought me messages that he would return at once, and accordingly in about three weeks, true to his promise, he once more presented himself.*

A system of division of profits at the end of the Chinese year exists throughout all China, even the smallest regular contributor to a shop's business participating in the profits, so that Lam Chong though in no way squeezing my purse, gets a small dividend through dealing at particular shops.

At the present moment there is a Javanese boy, Allitian by name, a most all round useful and excellent servant, who is lost to our sight somewhere in the centre of that thickly populated island. When we return, we will give general orders to all the Javanese we come in contact with for him to return to us. He owes us some $20 for which we hold no security whatever, but we fully expect to see him within three months of our return to Sandakan.[39]*

The head-house boy, Kai Yip, is a man of about 45, of a most stately and commanding presence; his personal appearance is a matter of great importance to him, and whenever he accompanies us out to a dinner party (in the East one always takes one's boy with one when dining out) attracts general admiration. He always wears fine silk coats of a pale french grey, and his feet and ankles are neatly clothed in ornamental Chinese shoes and stockings. His one passion is flowers; his methods for making plants grow are peculiar, he mixes human hair as well as feathers in the soil, and utilizes the entrails of fish and fowls besides other things, and even the water in which the day's supply of fish is cleaned is turned to account. The effects are undoubted, anything he manipulates thrives and blossoms in a surprising manner. To see him perambulating the garden in the cool of the morning arrayed in a huge Chinese hat some three feet in diameter, a tart fruit bottle half full of milk in one hand which he thumps 300 times in the palm of the other to produce butter, whilst he stops and gazes on his particular pets is indeed an amusing sight. Usually when we are taking our early coffee he brings us a flower or plant to admire, which he designates as being a "welly beauty piecee." His enthusiasm is carried to such lengths that even after a heavy night's rain, in the early morning he yet may be seen going round with a watering pot, having a theory that night rain contains salt which will damage the plants and must be washed off. I shall

---

*   The Javanese boy, Allitian, referred to has since returned to us as anticipated.

never forget his disgust at a new flower which he had imported at some trouble from Penang and brought into bloom after some months of care, as being "too muchee fooloo piecee, alla have spoilum" was his verdict when they all drooped and faded so that he was unable to use them for a dinner table decoration. His table decorations are very tasteful, his only failing being a weakness for too much mingling of colour, but when I venture to suggest any modification, the only reply I can get is "that no belong China custom."

One of my chief difficulties in life is getting the clothes washed. It is a perpetual fight and struggle with the Dhobie (washerman) be he Kling or Chinese: if the weather is fine the excuse for keeping the clothes for a most unwarrantable time – 3 or 4 weeks is nothing unusual – is, that the stream has been fouled by the piggeries, if the weather has been raining the water is muddy, or the clothes won't dry, there is always something; perhaps he has not had money to buy charcoal to heat the irons, it does not matter what the excuse is there is a stereotyped list of them. The mode of cleansing clothes is not conducive to their longevity. They are beaten and slashed on stones in the bed of a stream, if the Dhobie is so considerate as to use a board in lieu of a stone to whack the clothes upon, he is accounted a most considerate man; this is not all, they have a most objectionable habit of augmenting their incomes by renting out one's clothes to other persons whose wardrobes are not so extensive; this I believe to be the real reason why it is so difficult to get the clothes back when once the Dhobie has become possessed of them.

There is *always* something lost or spoilt, that goes as a foregone conclusion. On one occasion I recollect saying casually to the Dhobie "what have you spoilt this time?" "This time" he replied "it is the mosquite curtain" and to my dismay, sure enough I found the whole of one side mangled and haggled to pieces. It appeared that the Dhobie had washed it and laid it out on the grass to dry; there were some very bad goats there who desired to eat the grass, and to get at it they had to eat through the curtain, hence the mangled remains brought to me.

Ladies are all victims to the tyranny of Durzies (India tailors) there being no choice but to employ them, for the Chinese* tailors are utterly incapable of manufacturing ladies' garments, whereas these Indians, if one can but persuade them to do it are very clever at any kind of work, and will make any garment, lady's or gentlemen's, cover umbrellas, hats, make curtains,

---

* Since writing the above, a little Cantonese tailor has set up in business here and has proved himself a deliverer from the persecutions of the Dhurzies.

cover chairs and in a word do anything and everything. Their work too is always beautifully neat. It is strange at first to see these men squatting on a mat in the verandah busily cutting out a dress, making use of their toes as well as their hands in the operation. They are mean-spirited creatures, and if they once get you in their debt, woe betide you; you never can get any work out of them again, while on the other hand if you refuse to lend them money they will sit down in a corner of the verandah, rub their eyes till their tears come, and bother you to such an extent that at last you weakly yield. The contrast between their moral attributes and those of the Malays and Chinese is very great.

Their costume is a sort of white night dress curiously fashioned, beneath which they wear wide white cotton trousers ornamented with embroidery; perched on their greasy black locks which hang in tight corkscrew curls, a sort of meat-safe arrangement by way of a cap, completes their get up.

In houses surrounded by jungle the advent of day is proclaimed by a pretty gurgling sound as of running water, which is in reality nothing but the call of the wah-wah ape, this is followed by the loud shout of the argus pheasant, and the mournful cry of a bird that utters a peculiar sound, three notes on a descending scale. Then all the day insects waken up and begin their songs, the cicada most noticeable amongst the crowd.

The most enjoyable time of the whole day is the early morning; during the hours from 6 to 8 a.m. a delightful breeze blows, the sun shines and sheds a glory everywhere, and its heat does not become uncomfortable until 9 o'clock or so.

It is the custom of most persons to rise at day break and take a light breakfast of coffee, eggs, toast and fruit; the early morning is usually spent in the garden, in interviewing the cook and superintending household matters. A great many people take rides and walks while the day is still cool.

The office hours are from ten to four, after which time the European population disperses to lawn tennis, riding, billiards, and other amusements. Dinner parties, and occasionally dances, follow. It would be rather a novel sight for any one, not used to Eastern life, to see us start for a dinner party, the lady in ordinary evening costume, but the gentleman (supposing it is not a Government House dinner, at which function black dress is *de rigueur*) is arrayed in white duck trousers, short white mess jacket and bright hued cummerbund in lieu of a waistcoat. The lady's conveyance is a light bamboo sedan chair, slung on two long slender poles, which are borne on the shoulders of a couple of stout Canton coolies; Chinese lanterns are suspended before and behind, the boy leads the procession with another lantern, and his master's shoes tied up in a silk pocket handkerchief, the lady in her chair follows, and the gentleman brings up the rear on pony back. It is customary in the East when dining out to take your boy with you to wait upon you at table, a very excellent plan. The swinging motion when being carried in a chair is not an unpleasant one if the coolies are chair carriers by profession, but if they are not accustomed to the work, it is almost as bad as being at sea, added to which one has the idea that the bearers are being oppressed by one's weight. I have often been carried by comparatively small men quite easily, whereas stronger men sometimes labour and struggle with palpable distress, the whole secret being that the former understood their business whilst the others did not. They prefer to go at a good jog trot, and it is surprising how fast they can travel with their bare feet.

No form of entertainment in the East is more enjoyable than a moonlight pic-nic on a large and comfortable steam launch, provided the night be calm and fine; the Bay of Sandakan is perfect for a trip of this sort owing to its large size, and many inlets and pretty islands, verdure-clad to the waters' edge. Some nights it is almost as bright as day, and with a delicious breeze blowing, it is very cool and refreshing. One of the chief and most beautiful features is the phosphorescence in the water, which at certain periods is much brighter than at others. I have seen the Bay turn apparently milky white, the track of every fish, even the tiniest, denoted by a line of light, and the ripplets made by the bow of the launch cutting through the water being like pale blue liquid fire, at other times the whole horizon is one series of twinkling blue lights; experienced sailors have told me that no where else have they seen phosphorescence so bright, and beautiful as in Sandakan Harbour.

Chapter XIII.
Miscellaneous.

Snakes, scarcety of.—Adventure with.—Wild pigs.—Native dogs.—
Centipedes.—Wild animals.—Rhinoceros.—Adventure with.—
Orangutan.—Three shot.—Crocodile.—Man eaten by.—Dragon
procession.—Chinese funeral.—Shops.—Chit system.—Treasury
notes.—Anecdote.—Bamboo.—Rattans.—Turtles.—Turtle eggs.—
Wild turkey eggs.—Agar-agar.—Sea bathing.—Ikan buntal.—
Birds.—Hornbills.—Flower show.—Vegetables.

There seems to be a general impression, that wherever you turn in tropical countries, you are bound to come face to face with a snake. I have a friend who used to think that I found one under my pillow every night. I don't know how it may be in other countries, but snakes are quite scarce in North Borneo; I do not suppose, though we lived virtually on the borders of the jungle I have seen more than half a dozen all the time I have been here during a period of ten years; none of these were poisonous ones.

Once however I had rather an alarm, I went to look for an empty wine box, intending to convert it into a footstool, and on looking inside it, saw what I thought was a piece of oil cloth, wondering where this could have come from I looked more closely, and found that it was a snake curled up asleep. I quickly shut down the cover and shrieked for W. who came, captured it with a noose and transferred it to a bottle of spirits. The horrid thing had been visiting my fowls' nests and had swallowed five eggs, which were clearly visible owing to the way the body bulged at intervals.

The reason why there are not more snakes, is the abundance of wild pigs which eat them, hence ridding us of a nuisance, though they themselves we regard with no friendly eye, for the ravages they commit in the vegetable gardens are most distressing. It is also rather alarming, when coming home at night fall, to hear a crashing and crackling in the dry undergrowth, as a big pig runs away from the close neighbourhood of the garden gate. Some of the boars have very long tusks as compared with those from the Malay States. They are great enemies to the Sulus on our estate as they do much damage to their paddy fields and banana patches, and often of a morning one hears wild yells and the yapping of a pack of dogs in the forest, and knows that a pig hunt is in progress. The native and town dogs are very clever, forming parties on their own account for hunting, we used often to see them trot by our house to attend the meet without anybody being with them at all. European dogs do not make good pig hunters, they are too plucky and get terribly ripped and scored about, while the native dogs always take care to keep out of danger, but they always kill and eat the pigs they once settle down in chase of, and capture.

What I have more fear of than snakes and regard with more aversion, are centipedes, these are of the largest most loathsome type. They are not infrequently to be met with in the houses, especially if repairs to roof or walls be in progress. Their bite is very painful and causes great swellings. They are wonderfully active and seem to have an innate knowledge that man is their natural enemy, and disappear down a crack in the floor or other crevice with astonishing celerity when once perceived. Scorpions are also nasty things and their sting is even more painful, but they luckily are not so common.

There are a good many animals of one kind and another in the forest, monkeys, squirrels and so forth, beside the larger game; if one keeps chickens it is soon realized that there are many more animals than are usually supposed, for if one has not got two or three dogs about, musangs, civit cats, big monitor lizards up to eight feet long, snakes, rats and all manner of vermin are constantly making inroads on the poultry yard. There is no harm in any of these animals as far as one is concerned, and in fact the musangs can even be partly tamed.

But there are larger animals in the forest. We have had deer bound across our garden, and on one occasion a rhinoceros frequented a gully at the back of our house for two or three nights running, the dryness of the season having lured him down to our water supply, as they are fond of bathing. We wondered the first night what the loud grunting noise was, and stood on the verandah to hear him crashing amongst the herbage down below, whenever he came across a log in his path, against which he knocked his shins in the darkness, he swore after rhinoceros fashion and grumbled. One night he actually came up the water coolies' path, and made his way along the hill top towards the town, but when he turned the corner and saw lights ahead he became alarmed, and returned to his accustomed haunts: his peregrinations were clearly traceable next morning. They went after him two or three times but failed to come up with him, though they found a pool all muddy which he had lately been bathing in.

Just before we left Borneo W. stumbled across three in the forest, and had to get up a tree to escape from one, having no gun with him, but directly afterwards, his boy rushing up with the necessary fire arm, he pursued one and killed it. They are nasty ugly brutes but have not so far displayed any of those vices with which they are accredited.

The animal most peculiar to Borneo is the orang-utan: a family of three came down to the edge of the forest close to our house once. W. and I were returning from the estate to our house, when we saw a little group of Sulus below a tree, into whose top they were all gazing intently. It appeared that when they sent up the youngest of their party to get some fruit (the tree being in bearing) he almost went into the arms of the horrible animal. That boy came down much more quickly than he went up, but the poor creature only tried to hide itself in the leafy crest of the tree. We should not have touched it as they are harmless brutes, but it is very unpleasant to have them for such near neighbours, so I went for W.'s gun, and he shot it. It was a dreadfully hideous beast, enough to give one the nightmare, with a ferocious expression of countenance of which the stuffed specimens in museums give no adequate idea. This was the male, a few days later he shot the mother and child, they were not half so ugly. A curious feature about these animals is that they seem to contract lasting unions, and always go about in families of three, father, mother and child.

The Chinese have a strange infatuation for all sorts of extraordinary things, which they use as medicines, rhinoceros horns and the gall of the orangutan being amongst them, to obtain either one or other they will pay high prices.

The most ferocious creature we have is the crocodile, and he certainly is to be feared. Rarely a month passes but news reaches us that some one or other has been killed by one: they are most audacious and come right up to the town. Not long before we left, a China-man picking up drift wood on the shore was seized by one of these brutes, which proceeded to drag him away; his loud cries however caused his friends to rush to his rescue, and he was recovered, but in a very mauled condition; this happened just below the house we were living in at the time, which was situated in the centre of the town and we heard his cries plainly.

One of our men at Pulo Bai went out fishing with his son at night time in a long "gobang" (canoe). The boy went to sleep, but was suddenly awakened by the boat tipping over; he cried to his father but got no answer, and the father has never been heard of or seen since; no doubt a crocodile upset the boat and carried the man off. This old man had shortly before brought me some charms, which he said would preserve the bearer from harm, as W. was going on an expedition which involved danger; it was owing to the absence of these charms that his friends attributed the occurrence.

From crocodiles to dragons is but a short step. Our Chinese sometimes indulge in very fine dragon feasts, the dragon being 150 feet long. This creature has a huge and grotesque head, the body is composed of many yards of coloured silk fastened round the ribs, each rib being supported by a man. The mouth is immense and open, and it has great goggle eyes. A man carries a ball in front of it which it is supposed to be pursuing. As the procession passes along, the owners of the houses which line the way, fling out lighted crackers which make a great noise and smoke, and the dragon pretends to revel in the fire, wagging its head and opening and shutting its mouth as though devouring the smoke. It is attended by bands, playing the most excruciating music, and all sorts of other extraordinary arrangements are carried behind it. All this seeming child's play affords the greatest interest to our celestial neighbours.

While on the subject of processions, I will describe one that I met, it turned out to be the funeral of a well known Chinaman who had died of heart disease. First came a band, followed by persons carrying baskets in which were a large supply of square pieces of paper in the centre of which were dabs of gold and silver, these they scattered to right and left as they went along, the object being that the evil spirits, in their greed for wealth, would seize these and be so much occupied with them, that they would not have time to molest the spirit of the deceased. Then came what appeared to be a huge bolster covered with coarse sacking, upon the top of which a white cock, tied by the leg, fluttered about, much objecting to the situation. This must have been the coffin; the object of the cock being there was that he might fight any demon which tried to interfere with the spirit. For my part I should think the bands of the departed weird music, and the loud incessant beating of instruments, which emitted a din like children playing on tin tea trays (Chinese gongs) much more likely to frighten them away.

The shops in Sandakan are quite open in the front, there are no windows at all, consequently all their goods are exposed to view. The shop-keepers squat on platforms which do duty instead of counters, or stand on them to reach down the various articles for inspection. At night the whole shop front is closed by shutters. All the every day necessaries of life are obtainable in these shops, or at the stores kept by Europeans, of which there are three or four.

What is known as the chit system in China is usually adopted in North Borneo, no one ever thinks of carrying about the cumberous silver dollars of Mexico and Japan which are current, and instead, whenever anything is bought, all one does is to give the shop-keeper an I.O.U. for its value. At the end of the month, these are all brought in for payment. There is very little small silver currency, and our transactions of less than a dollar are conducted in North Borneo cents. They are packed in rolls of 50 which are very cumbersome and weighty.

British North Borneo notes are issued by the Treasury the values being

$1., $5. and $25. These save a good deal of inconvenience, a $25. note being no trouble to carry, while that number of dollars is exceedingly heavy.

On one occasion an astute Malay from foreign parts practised a mean trick upon some of our unsophisticated natives living beyond the centre of civilization. This man took one of the labels out of a Huntley and Palmers' biscuit box and palmed it off as a $25. note, it being of somewhat the same size and appearance, and having reproductions of prize medals upon it which looked like stamps to our credulous and bucolic friends: complaint was made to W. about it, and he had the man captured and gave him two years' imprisonment.

Bamboos throughout the East are most useful, being adapted for endless purposes, amongst them is that of doing duty for a water bucket, a good large one with knots far apart, is often employed for this purpose and is carried over the shoulder.[40] Rattans are also equally useful, as rope, string and ties, in lieu of nails, for house building. Large kinds in the interior are even used as flooring for houses.

The islands off the coast are frequented by turtles, which are preserved, as their eggs form quite an item of the people's food supply. These turtles go ashore at night and scratch holes in the sand, in which they lay a lot of eggs, whereupon the natives who have been on the look out, go, and collect them all and bring them to Sandakan, where they are sold by hundreds in the Fish Market. The right to collect these eggs is reserved as a Government Monopoly, and granted to chief men amongst the Bajows, as before this system was adopted the collection of these eggs led to much quarrelling, and even fighting. The eggs are round and soft, the shell not being hard like that of a hen's egg, but tough and leathery, so that wherever one touches them they become indented. I could never summon up courage to try them but I have been told they are good in omelettes.

The eggs of a small wild turkey are collected in a somewhat similar manner. These turkeys make huge nests formed of twigs, earth, leaves and grass, into a sort of mound about 15 ft. across, in the middle of which they bury their eggs. These are of course nothing like so numerous as those of the turtle but their nests are to be found all along the coast line. These eggs are very large, as compared to the size of the bird, and are very good eating.

Agar-agar is a sort of sea weed, much like Iceland moss I should imagine; it is found in coral seas, is a greeny hue when first collected, but turns white when dried and bleached. It abounds in our seas and may be collected by the hundred weight. It is used to make a sort of jelly, but is not to be classed with isinglass and I do not like it. Cuttle fish, tripang or beche-de-mer, keema, besides sharks' fins, etc. are always being collected along the foreshore by the wandering Bajows.

Sea bathing is a pastime that can only be indulged in fear and trembling; not only are crocodiles and sharks to be apprehended, but the water is full of stinging medusae or jelly fish, whose trailers twist themselves round the rash bather and sting him with more or less severity. On two occasions I have known of native children having been stung to death by them, and to others they have occasioned great pain, and what between shells with sharp spines, a podgy black creature with numerous black thorns protruding, and fish that sting, wading in shallow water also has its drawbacks.

Amongst the many curious objects to be seen in the pools left by the receding tide, are queer little fish known as "ikan buntal;" whose mouths resemble parrots' beaks: when lifted out of the water they have the extraordinary power of blowing out their skins until they are as round as a ball, and as hard. When they blow off the air they do so with a little squeaking sound. Some of these fish grow to a foot and over in length.

There are not so many birds to be seen as might be supposed, nor are the bright plumaged ones the commonest, at the same time, now and again one gets an assurance that one is in the tropics by catching a glimpse of some gorgeously coloured specimen. One of the prettiest ones that is more often seen, is a little long-billed kind resembling a humming-bird, which is so tame that it builds its nest from stray rattan ends hanging down from the roof in the verandah, it has a bright metallic blue green head and yellow wings. These little birds are honey-eaters and we have often watched them while hovering about the great red flowery heads of a species of chlorodendron which grows luxuriantly in our garden, wage big sparring matches with large papilio butterflies who desire to sip the sweets from the same blossoms. I need hardly say that the bird with his long sharp formidable beak is of course always the victor. Amongst those commonest in the forest are large horn-bills which sit on the tops of trees beyond gun-shot, and utter the most discordant squawks and screams. They have enormous bills, out of all proportion to the size of their bodies, sometimes very brightly coloured, rosey pink and yellow. Their plumage is black pied with white. The Dyaks are very fond of using the heads of these birds with the bills, to decorate the front of their war caps, sticking the long tail feathers of the Argus pheasant through the crowns of them.

Once a year, usually at Chinese New Year, which is a moveable feast depending on the moon, but which always occurs early in our New Year, oftenest about February, a Flower show is held: this however does not cover all the facts of the case as in addition monkies, coral, bricks, bread, needlework, geese, fowls, native arms and Natural History specimens are shown, as well as small quantities of general produce such as coffee and sugar cane which latter usually attracts very marked praise as it is often exceedingly fine. Added to the above prizes are offered for fruit and vegetables. In fact anything and everything that anyone likes to bring can find admission.

The flowers as may be supposed make a very pretty and attractive show, the bouquets and table decorations are often very tasteful. The foliage plants, caladiums and coleuses, always command a foremost place, the ferns also often being very handsome. The show of pot-plants would always do greater credit to the various gardeners, were it not for the high rate of coolie labour which deters many from competing as they all have to be carried by hand, so that the prize winners only recoup their outlay, whilst the unsuccessful exhibitors are entirely out of pocket.

There is always keen competition amongst the market gardeners for the vegetable prizes. Our vegetables though not choice are numerous. I have seen as many as 36 kinds exhibited by one man, of which tomatoes, cucumbers, brinjals, and Chinese radishes were perhaps the best. As for our french beans they grow by the yard, four or five when cut up are sufficient for a dish.

The huge forest that covers the country consists of some six hundred different kinds of trees, which are mostly of great height, their crowns of leaves being often two hundred feet above the ground, while the enormous trunks spring up column-like some a hundred feet and more before the first branch spreads itself forth. Many of them have great buttresses proceeding from the main trunk near the ground, making recesses many feet deep. These trees nearly all afford timber of more or less value, and vary in quality from the hardest of hard woods down to some almost cork-like in their substance: among them there are a great variety of fruit trees, including several sorts of wild Mango, besides the Durian, Langsat, rambutan, and others, while two or three species of wild nutmeg are not uncommon on low flat lands. Considerable portions of the Coast are fringed with broad mangrove swamps, from the bark of which a valuable tanning material is obtained, whilst the wood is found to make good fuel for steam launches.

The usual idea of a tropical forest is somewhat wide of the mark, as, except for the size of the enormous trees, there is little difference between it and an English wood, the palm trees which are supposed to comprise the principal part of the vegetation being rarely seen. Perhaps what strikes one most is the presence of numbers of large creepers which at intervals interlace the trees. Amongst these the most useful is the rattan which is itself a palm, although very unlike the palm trees seen in conservatories in Europe, as its numerous stems are long, thin, leafless and thorny as far as one can see, the only leaves it has being merged in the general mass of foliage far overhead.

The forest, even at mid-day, when the sun is at its highest, is cool, gloomy and silent: at day break the monkeys call, and the myriads of insects raise a pleasant and not unmusical chorus, but beyond this and the occasional call of a bird very few sounds are heard.

There are but few really dangerous animals to be met with, although the rhinoceros, perhaps the most disagreeable of them, is far from uncommon, besides which there is also a small kind of bear but I have never heard of any one being hurt by either of these animals. Monkeys abound, from the large red-coated orangutan with his immense span of arm and tremendous muscular strength to the smallest ape; the most interesting of the latter being the kalawat, or wah-wah, whose pretty soft grey coat and shiny black face and funny wrinkled foreheads are the most attractive, their great black eyes always have a pleading look in them; they do not rebel in captivity if they are greatly petted, but quickly die if much attention is not bestowed upon them.

Elephants are not infrequently heard of but they are not by any means often seen: wild cattle, wild pigs and deer are not uncommon, the smallest of the latter being a very diminutive creature most delicately fashioned; it chiefly goes by the name of mouse-deer. It is generally caught in traps and its poor little legs being so slender, are often in consequence broken.

Of birds there are very many kinds including the handsome fire back and argus pheasants, gay plumaged pigeons of several varieties, partridges and many others, not omitting the bul-bul as well as a bird that has a strange mournful cry, five minor notes on a descending scale.

Perhaps the most unpleasant inhabitants of the forests are the leeches which swarm everywhere wriggling their thin ugly browny-yellow bodies from the tips of leaves, waiting some passing object whether man or beast to which to attach themselves. If the blood is not in good condition their bites cause much trouble, making sores which in some cases, do not heal for weeks. On the other hand, if the person bitten is in good health the leeches have but little effect on him. Mosquitoes there are, of course, and sandflies, the latter being perhaps the worse plague of the two but neither kind of these tiresome little flies can be said to be very plentiful except in certain localities. At nighttime the feathery clumps of bamboo and bracken are made beautiful by the lovely fireflies which flit about them flashing their bright rays of light at short intervals, reminding one forcibly of falling stars: glow worms are to be found on every bank and sometimes various kinds of fungi which emit a phosphorescent light, and even dead leaves may occasionally be met with which have the appearance of being covered with luminous paint.

There are not so many snakes as is generally imagined, sometimes it is true a big python is noosed and brought into town, while occasionally a slim grass green snake is seen gracefully winding its way through the bushes, or amongst the flowery creepers which form arches in our gardens, but they are quite harmless and as a matter of fact poisonous snakes are very rare, though, at long intervals, a hamadryad is reported; this latter is of course one of the most baneful, not only being provided with very poisonous fangs but also is one of the very few that sometimes shows a disposition to attack man. On a recent occasion a huge python having swallowed a deer which was distinctly observable in its body, was captured in a dormant condition on our land, and a case of the same kind occurred not long ago in the Ulu Kinabatangan. Each of these snakes was over twenty feet long, and although so large in size, yet the bodies of the animals devoured stood out in bold relief through the expanded skin, which was strained to such an extent that it was on the point of bursting.

A not uninteresting elephant hunt occurred not long ago on a newly opened estate. An elephant espying some young and succulent banana plants valiantly ventured into the clearing in the middle of the day. The coolies shouted and made demonstrations hoping thereby to frighten him away, but he refused to retreat and charged right at them: a fight thereupon ensued, the men prodding him with their woodknives and spears whilst the elephant chased them about. Finally, one man more valiant than the others, in the excitement of the encounter, sprang on to a great log and from thence on to the beast's back, from which point of vantage he succeeded in dividing one of the animal's spinal vertebrae.

Orangutans make platforms of branches and leaves in the forks of the trees, for their sleeping places. Two orangutans that I knew and which were kept in captivity for a long while were very amusing in their habits. Although they were half grown they were not kept in a cage or even chained, but lived quite happily and comfortably in a couple of small trees by the cook-house, and they were so tame that they would take their masters' hand and walk about with him. They were most deliberate in all their movements, scorning anything so undignified as haste. The male used often to amuse himself for hours by climbing to the top of the roof of the cook-house, and then in the most solemn sober manner, curl himself together and roll down like a ball. They had a very human way of shading the sun from their eyes when peering at an object in the distance, when the sun interfered with their view, placing their spread hands in a slow contemplative manner across their foreheads as a man would do under similar circumstances.

It was very odd to watch them when rain came, try to cover their heads with a handful of long grass as a protection against the downpour, but what they liked better for this purpose was an old kerosine oil tin, and if there happened to be one lying anywhere about, it was esteemed a great treasure and a most enviable defence against a tropical shower. I have seen the male snatch one of these tins in a most ungallant manner from his wife. In fact the poor little lady had generally rather a rough time of it, her husband not having been remarkable for his kindness to her, he would greedily snatch anything she was eating from her in a very ungentlemanly fashion, while she, poor thing, submitted meekly like an ill-used wife whimpering only a pitiful protest. At one time he gobbled up the food so fast that she was a quite disreputable object, being so poorly nourished, and for this reason the male was at last chained up. When she died however, her widower greatly mourned her loss, took to sadly intemperate habits and finally, after no long period, succumbed to the combined effects of remorse, grief and intemperance.

There are many lovely butterflies of great varieties, from the large transparent ghost butterfly which slowly flaps about in gloomy places, and the richly coloured black and yellow ornithoptera, a span's breadth across the wings, to the tiny blues with their delicate markings which flicker over every bank of flowers. The moths which fly into the houses at night time are no less beautiful and their varieties exceed even those of the butterflies.

Orchids abound, though they are not so easily obtainable nor so often seen in blossom as seems to be generally supposed, and unless a patch of jungle is being felled, whether for timber purposes or for planting, they are very difficult to get. The greater proportion of them are very small and insignificant, but we have some that would delight the hearts of orchid collectors at home, the most beautiful being the *phalaenopsis amabalis*, and two other kinds whose names I do not know have been acquired up the rivers in Sandakan Bay; their flowers are very much alike in character but their leaves and bulbs quite different each from the other.

The curious pitcher plants can be found anywhere where there is dry sandy soil and begonias thrive in the vicinity of lime stone rocks.

Orchid collecting is not quite such easy work as those at a distance may suppose. Labels are not attached by nature to orchids as they grow in the forest, as many people in England from the way they write would seem to think, and as many of them very closely resemble one another, it is provoking, after carefully pampering for some months a sort which looks as though it ought to have fine large handsome blossoms, to find it results in flowers of almost microscopical dimensions. Nor is this the only awkwardness. Difficulties of all kinds arise in orchid collecting; the following is an instance. My husband's brother who visited us some years ago wrote back to us saying that he had identified an orchid he saw in the forest as a very valuable species and giving us directions where to find it. After a little exploring it was discovered at the place referred to, at the extreme top of a high tree. It looked large but not particularly so. My husband ordered the tree to be cut down, which was done with the unfortunate result that it fell upon a government bridge on the main road about 150 feet off, smashing it entirely.

The orchid itself, a grammatophyllum, when we got close to it we found was large enough to fill a couple of carts, it was knocked all to fragments however by the fall, but some of these – several men's loads – we carried off and placed in a gully at the back of the house in the hope that they would strike, but that night there was very heavy rain and next morning not a vestige of it remained, so there was an end of that orchid and all the expense connected with it, and all we had to do was to build another bridge.

The weather is sometimes rough but the winds never freshen to a gale, and for the most part I am told it is very pleasant to cruise about in these waters; (being an exceptionally bad sailor myself, I unluckily cannot endorse this opinion). At mid-day, when the sun is shining, the white sandy beaches dotted with little native houses, backed by luxuriant foliage, with the bright green and blue coral shaded water lapping the shore, forms a bright and pleasant picture. On calm still nights, usually towards the close of the year, the phosphorescence is so great that the waters of the Bay turn a milky white, with brilliant fiery lights glowing here and there where the fish or a boat breaks up the sea into riplets. Beneath the tiny wavelets bloom perfect sea-gardens with banks of blue, green, yellow and red and other colours ruled by the pre-dominating shade of the masses of coral, whilst among them flit fish of brilliant hues, turquoise blue to vivid scarlet.

The most terrible scourge we have in Borneo is the crocodile. This cruel monster which in most other countries occurs in fresh water only, is often with us found far out to sea, and there are one or two species which never seek fresh water at all. Other kinds on the contrary keep to the rivers only, inhabiting and abounding in the shallow lagoons at the back of the main rivers. The sea is so full of sharks that their fins salted and sundried form a main article of trade in some places.

There is a remarkable absence of unpleasant natural phenomena in

North Borneo, volcanos and earthquakes are quite unknown on the East Coast, and typhoons never reach us. The volcanic belt passes round to the eastward of us some hundreds of miles, but I may record here that the Krakatoa eruption in August 1883 was distinctly heard at Sandakan notwithstanding that the scene of it lies no less than 1,200 miles away, whilst so recently as 7th June, 1892 we again heard heavy muffled explosions which were at once pronounced by some persons to be caused by an eruption. This proved to be true as we afterwards were informed that an eruption had taken place on the evening of that day at Sangir Island nearly 600 miles to the east of us.

As far as is known there are but few minerals or metals in Borneo. Coal outcrops occur in two or three places especially in the S.W. district, while the existence of gold in the upper Segama has been long known; the following extract from Dalrymple no doubt refers to it. "Unsang; this district produces plenty of very fine gold which is soft like wax; the most remarkable for this is Talassam, within Giong, but the river disembogues in the North Sea between Tambisan and Sandakan."

It was while on a journey up the Segama, undertaken at my husband's request, in search of the gold district referred to in the above extract, that the unfortunate Frank Hatton met his death while elephant shooting (he was the first European to put a bullet in a Bornean elephant); his sad death brought the expedition to a summary close. Had he lived, no doubt years ago, the whole question of the real value of the gold deposits in North Borneo would have been determined.

Slavery though not absolutely prohibited by law is largely restricted and has almost died a natural death: since 1883 all children born of slave parents have been free. W. on his first advent in the country had great difficulty in making the people understand that there was any other condition than that of slavery.

It must not be supposed that slavery in these parts partook of anything after the "Uncle Tom's Cabin" form, there were no overseers, long whip in hand, to stand over gangs of men and crack them up with a long lash, no tracking of runaway men and women by blood hounds, slaves were often as well if not better clothed than their masters and loafed through life much in the same lazy manner, and if hard work was demanded of them they thought themselves very ill-used, in fact they considered that the *raison d'être* of a master was before all things to support his slaves in comfort.[41]

The footing on which they stood with their masters may be gathered from the following entry in W.'s diary of 14th October 1878. "Bought Juan of Mohamed Ascalee for $90, told him he was a free man which he seemed to regard from the heritage of woe point of view and was very melancholy about it. Mohamed addressed a few words to him on handing him over and then burst into tears. Juan wept and Mohamed's wife howled, altogether it was most affecting."

It was difficult to make them comprehend the dignity of freedom. One man who W. freed, on being met with after some months later, was discovered again as a slave. On enquiry it turned out that he had sold himself for a concertina with which he wanted to capture the affections of a young native lady. On another occasion a man came to W. for advice about a slave; she would not sew, she refused to cook, she would do nothing but sit in the verandah and chew sirih. W. advised the master to cut down her rations, but this was no use, she went and helped herself when the food was prepared. W. then suggested he had better sell the woman, but here again occurred a difficulty, for no one could be found bold enough to buy her or even take her as a gift, so bad a reputation did she bear. It was then proposed that the master should turn her out of the house, but this was no use as there are no front doors, so she simply walked in again. As a last and extreme resource W. hinted that perhaps he might even go so far as to administer a little very mild correction but this was courting a climax. In half an hour, in rushed the master with a very disordered appearance and blood streaming down his face. He said that would never do as she was the stronger and beat him instead.

CHAPTER XIV.
COFFEE PLANTING.

Gigantic trees.—Price of felling.—Land selecting.—Selups and rentices.—Seed beds.—Mode of tree felling.—Axes.—Native labour.—Chaos.—Burning off.—Building.—Holeing and lining.—Planting.—Liberian coffee.

Work in connection with the opening of an estate or plantation of any kind is very interesting. To a person unused to agricultural operations in the tropics, as he stands in the primeval forest and glances around him, noting the size and circumference of the giant trees which seem to defy the puny strength of flesh and muscle, the hope and desire to convert such a tract of forest into smiling districts of food producing land, or into waving fields of yellow paddi or sweet scented coffee gardens, seems almost appalling and well nigh impossible.

Gazing above and around him he sees trees varying in size from the thickness of his arm to a diameter of five feet and perhaps even more, springing up straight and columnlike to a height of 200 feet overhead, whilst the ground at his feet is a tangle of roots. The prospect in truth is not encouraging, and indeed many Chinamen, who have at one time or another been attracted to Borneo on the promise of cheap fertile land, have after a single walk in the silent and gloomy forest depths fled back to China straightway, while even Englishmen not used to it, frequently look upon the task of merely felling those forest monsters as the work of a giant endowed with super-human powers, and have devised steam felling machines and other such appliances for the more sure and speedy felling of such trees, whereas for four dollars an acre, any number of Malay gang foreman can be found to undertake contracts to lay it low, the charge for an acre, being I suppose, not much more than English labourers would demand for felling a single tree, and yet these huge trees stand close together and our virgin forests hold often twenty of such to an acre to say nothing of the hundreds of from one to two feet thick.

We will suppose that it is a coffee estate that is to be the scene of operations. Naturally the first thing is to select the land. In North Borneo this is not a very difficult matter, the required description of ground existing almost everywhere, long undulating hillocks as near sea level as possible. Care must also be taken to select the land on the banks of a navigable river in order to ensure cheap transport, whilst a most important point to be kept in mind is not to be at any great distance from your base of supplies, upon which the price of rice and provisions for the coolies greatly depends, a matter which may make just the difference between a profit and a loss in the days to come. Given those advantages, if exactly the proper description of soil can be combined, the planter can start work without misgivings.

Arrived at this point, it is usual to engage a gang of men on day wages, and the exact spot for the commencement having been settled upon, a small clearing in the forest is made. Here are run up hastily a series of leantos, "selups" as they are called, diminutive mat sheds long and narrow, raised above the ground on poles with the ever useful Kadjangs mats thrown over them. Selups for twenty men can easily be made in a day. A rough shelter having thus been made, the next morning the planter throws his men into the forest with orders to cut long straight lines or lanes known technically as "rentices," with again other "rentices" at right angles at distances of every two hundred yards, thus cutting up the block into a series of squares like a chess board of little over eight acres each, which are known locally as "pajuks."

The blocks having thus been marked out, the next thing is to make contracts for the felling of these "pajuks," the price depending upon the nearness to the town of the forest and usually ranging from $26 to $32 each, a contractor taking two to four such "pajuks" according to the size of his gang. The cleverest fellers in North Borneo are either Bornean Malays, Kadyans or Sooloos.

It is considered by most planters advisable to leave strips of low forest standing some thirty or forty feet broad in two or three directions to act as wind screens.

Matters having progressed thus far, the next care of the planter is directed to his seed beds; unless he has been able to secure promise of the necessary young plants he proceeds to prepare nurseries (beebits) with as little delay as possible, as the coffee beans take eight to nine months from the time they are put in, until they are strong young plants ready for the fields.

The forest felling gangs at once get to work; first of all armed only with their long wood knives known as "parangs." These implements are of different shapes, but are usually curved or scimeter shaped blades some eighteen inches in length, with which they cut over all the small undergrowth, saplings and young trees up to four and five inches thick; this done over the whole block of land, they next attack the larger trees up to two feet or so in diameter; now heavier tools become necessary, either a light American axe or more often their own "billiongs," insignificant little weapons to look at, hatchet shaped, bound with rattan to a long thin pliable piece of wood made of a root for handle, which bites deep into the hearts of all but the hardest of hard woods.

By this time there remain standing but the giants of the forest, trees measuring frequently up to six feet and even more in diameter, many of them having buttresses reaching out on all sides and stretching up to a height often of twelve feet from the ground: above these buttresses the forest fellers proceed to erect a light staging or platform upon which they take their stand, attacking the tree on opposite sides. Seen thus, the men seem very pigmies as compared with the great monster they are about to attack and their weapons utterly unfitted for such work of destruction; but see, the arms are already lifted high, the little "billiongs" are already at work, and a sound reaches the ear while the chips of wood fly right and left, those sharp little axes are already beginning to eat their way into the heart of the giant with astonishing rapidity.

After an hour's work, or it may be more, according to the size of the tree and the quality of the wood, a faint crackling sound is detected by experienced ears; the fellers proceed with more caution and strike with less rapidity, for that was a note of warning and the end is not far off. After chipping with care and a listening ear, one of the men descends from the platform while his comrade continues his tapping, pausing frequently to listen for ominous sounds such as his accustomed ear quickly detects. At last a louder cracking sound is heard, the fibres begin to strain, and throwing aside his axe the wood man utters a wild yell of warning, hastily clambers down from his platform and escapes to a place of safety with all the agility of a nimble squirrel.

The tree top sways and bends his leafy crown, the branches shiver, the crackling sounds augment, the mighty crest bows and bends, and then with an increasing rushing sound and a terrific crash falls to the ground making it shake amidst the exultant yells of the excited Sooloos.

This feat successfully accomplished, unlike an English labourer who would require a tankard of ale to refresh his exhausted system after such a spell of hard work, the small lithe natives squat on their heels on a prostrate log, and roll up and smoke a cigarette while they calmly contemplate the surrounding trees and decide which one they will next attack.

Often they will half cut through a number of trees, and then fell one larger and heavier than the rest in such a clever manner as to bring them all down together; at other times they will, as it were, take aim with one tree at another and turn it over roots and all, without having even touched it with their axe.

The felling concluded, the scene is now one of the wildest wreck and confusion: huge trees lying one over another in all directions, while an impenetrable tangle of broken branches, boughs and leaves six feet or so deep covers the ground, so that it is only possible to get about at all by passing from one prostrate tree trunk to another, which it needs a nimble and experienced foot to accomplish in safety.

To a novice, introduced now to such a scene of chaos, with instructions that he is to evolve an orderly well planted coffee estate upon the site of havoc and confusion before him, the effect is almost appalling, it seeming all but an impossibility even to get the ground cleared of such tons of timber.

In the case of opening a coffee estate, it is usual to wait until a spell of hot sunny weather shall have made the whole mass of leaves and branches so dry that the fire will easily spread and run, so devouring them all without artificial aid and even to some extent burning off the larger logs which hamper the ground, or leaving them to smoulder away slowly. It is a most impressive sight to see a large acreage being devoured by fire in this manner. Enormous tongues of flame leap up thirty and forty feet in the air, vast columns of smoke ascend and darken the sky, while the intense heat, loud crackling and sputtering noises of the flames consuming the huge logs of wood is quite awful. I speak of an area, as large as that occupied by St. James' Park, one sea of flames. Owing to the humidity under the forest shade these fires never extend into the surrounding district as might be anticipated.

The time has now arrived when it becomes necessary to think about the erection of more roomy and comfortable quarters for the staff, from Manager to coolies, and house building is taken in hand. The selection of suitable sites for the new habitations is most important, and rising or hilly ground should be chosen, but as a rule sufficient attention to this most important point is not given, and too often they are made on the flat, which in rainy seasons becomes damp and unhealthy and is the cause of much sickness.

Clearing is the next operation after burning; if the latter has been a good one this is soon finished, but in wet weather or with a bad burn, it becomes one of the most expensive operations connected with planting.

It will be understood that even the best burn still leaves large logs 100 feet in length and more, lying piled upon the ground, while the stumps, many of them of huge size, still remain standing all over the estate waiting the process of slow decay, (ploughing is of course quite out of the question) but they are not, as a rule, found to interfere much with the next process, that of holeing and lining, which is done by a good many couples holding out stretched lines crossed by other similar lines the same distance apart eight to nine feet. Whenever the lines cross, a wooden peg is put in to indicate the spots where the holes are to be made in which the coffee seedlings will be planted. Eight and a half feet is considered to be the best distance apart by most planters.

The lining finished, contracts are then usually given to Chinese to dig so many holes, usually eighteen inches broad by eighteen inches deep; after which these holes are filled with surface earth mingled with the wood-ash produced by the burning of the forest. All is now ready for planting which is usually proceeded with when a period of two or three successive days' rain has made the ground thoroughly damp.

I suppose every planter differs slightly in his mode of conducting this operation, but the one object in view is of course to put in as strong and healthy plants as can be procured, giving them the best advantages possible. Whether you shade them more or less, or whether the tap-root is stumped or not, whether you use a parang or a hoe or the hands for planting, are all methods which vary according to the idea of the planter.

The estate now planted up, the planter, like the farmer at home, proceeds according to my experience to grumble at the weather whatever it may be. The coffee shows its first blossom when it is about eleven months of age, and yields its first cherries in about its twentieth month.

Liberian coffee is always a fine handsome plant with its large dark green leaves and its big jassmine like flowers and exquisite perfume, after a spell of rainy weather it throws out a flush of pure white blossoms which make it still more attractive.

These flushes of bloom do not occur at any stated intervals but seem to come out all the year round, whenever the weather is favourable, the consequence is that on the same shrub, flowers and the cherry in all stages from tiny pea like berries, up to the ripe scarlet berry are to be seen.

CHAPTER XV.
CONCLUSION.

Hopes and aims.—Minerals.—Frank Hatton.—The soil the country's chief mainstay.—Comparison with Java and the Philippines.—Resources still undeveloped.

The end that W. had in view from the first beginning of all things, and from which he has never for a moment wavered was to get the country into such a peaceful and orderly state that capitalists should be attracted to develop its resources, as it was not the intention of the Association first, or of the B. N. Borneo Co. afterwards, to do more themselves than administer the country.

It was at first hoped that minerals would be found, and steps were at once taken to discover what minerals or metals there were. To this end, Frank Hatton was engaged to explore the country, the story of his travels, researches and untimely end are related fully elsewhere.* He went very thoroughly over a good deal of the country and left but little doubt but that, if there were any metals to speak of, they would require much closer examination to bring to light, than he was commissioned to make, a conclusion which time has only tended to confirm.[42]

This being the case, there only remained as the country's mainstay, the fertility of its soil, the enormous acreage, concentrating upon some of the finest harbours in the world and the healthiness of its climate. It was quite certain that these, especially in the Sandakan district were unquestionable, and that these very evident advantages would attract attention seemed to W. only natural, that in fact Great Britain, which had hitherto not possessed any tropical colony possessing much fertility of soil, would seize with avidity the opportunity of developing the resources of a country that vied with the Philippines and Java in all their best points, lacking at the same time a good many of the disadvantages of those islands, seemed probable and he hoped that it would not be long before Borneo would begin to fulfil its obvious destiny of coming to the fore as one of the main producers of tropical commodities for the world, supporting a large and ever increasing population of its own, its one enormous stretch of forest gradually receding and giving place to fields and plantations of all kinds, while towns and villages slowly grew up of their own accord at the most suitable centres.

So far, these expectations have not been fulfilled, but it does not remain

---

*   *North Borneo, Explorations and Adventures on the Equator* with me to explain the reason and cause of this delay; suffice it to say, that the soil and natural advantages are not at fault. The vast agricultural resources remain intact, virtually undeveloped, notwithstanding the hundreds of thousands of acres of land adapted for sugar, coffee, Manila-hemp, cocoanuts and india rubber, and many other tropical products known to give very profitable results to the cultivator if only inaugurated in districts near to a port of shipment, for here (unlike Africa, where the fertile districts are far distant from the coast so that the cost of carriage to a port must necessarily be one of the chief items of calculation in connection with the export of produce), vast acreages centre on good shipping harbours, so that exports can be shipped off at the lowest possible expense.

The day cannot be far off, however, when North Borneo's enormous capabilities must perforce demand attention and attract notice to this the finest tropical agricultural country that Great Britain possesses.*

END.

* These lines were written in January, 1893.

EDITOR'S NOTES

1. Joseph Hatton, *The New Ceylon: Being a Sketch of British North Borneo, or Sabah* (London: Chapman and Hall, 1881). Joseph Hatton (1841–1907) was a popular and extremely prolific writer of all kinds of books, whose reputation extended to the United States as well as Great Britain. His writing the introduction to Pryer's little book brought some much-needed publicity to her endeavour.

2. Antonio Piggafetta, *The Last Voyage Around the World by Magellan*, 'Translated from the Account by Piggafetta' (London: Hakluyt Society, 1874).

3. Captain Daniel Beeckman visited Borneo in 1716. He published his account, *A Voyage to and from the Island of Borneo* (London: T. Warner and J. Batley) in 1718.

4. For a somewhat detailed history of imperial activity in the region in the nineteenth century, see Nicholas Tarling, *British Policy in the Malay Peninsula and Archipelago, 1824–71* (London: Oxford University Press, 1969).

5. What Ada Pryer refers to as *Dalton's Papers on Borneo* and as *Dyaks of Borneo* was actually published in Singapore in 1837, as 'Essay on the Diaks of Borneo', in *Notices of the Indian Archipelago and Adjacent Countries: Being a Collection of Papers Relating to Borneo, Celebes, Bali, Java, Sumatra, Nias, the Philippine Islands, Sulus, Siam, Cochin China, Malayan Peninsula, Etc.*, compiled by J. H. Moor. The book was reprinted in London by Cass in 1968.

6. Spencer St John, *The Life of Sir James Brooke, Rajah of Sarawak, from His Personal Papers and Correspondence* (Edinburgh: W. Blackwood and Sons, 1879).

7. See Nicholas Tarling, *Britain, the Brookes, and Brunei* (Kuala Lumpur: Oxford University Press, 1971).

8. Carl Bock, *The Headhunters of Borneo: A Narrative of Travel up the Mahakkam and down the Barito; also, Journeying in Sumatra* (1881; reprinted Singapore: Oxford University Press, 1985).

9. Captain Franz Xavier Witti was an Austrian. His private account of his last expedition to Borneo was published by G. C. Woolley, as 'Mr. F. X. Witti's

Last Journey and Death', *Bulletin of the North Borneo State Museum* (Sandakan, 1938).

10. For detailed histories of the British presence in North Borneo, particularly accounts which include not just the British perspective but the histories, views and positions of the local inhabitants as well, see Ulla Wagner, *Colonialism and Iban Warfare* (Stockholm: OBE Tryck, 1972), and James F. Warren, *The North Borneo Chartered Company's Administration of the Bajau, 1879–1909: The Pacification of a Maritime, Nomadic People* (Athens: Ohio University Center for International Studies, 1971).

11. In 1878 W. C. Cowie was a gun runner for the Sulus against the Spanish blockade. He accompanied Overbeck and Pryer to see the Sultan of Sulu in 1878, and may well have been helpful in persuading the Sultan to sign the concessions. After a rocky beginning, Cowie did throw his support behind the newcomer, Pryer, and the new company in Sandakan. In fact, this independent-minded entrepreneur was later to become head of the British North Borneo Company.

12. For a useful discussion of British notions of piracy, see Robert Pringle, *Rajahs and Rebels: The Ibans of Sarawak under Brooke Rule, 1841–1941* (Ithaca, NY: Cornell University Press, 1970).

13. Recall that, previous to coming to Borneo, William Pryer had worked in China.

14. For an illuminating analysis of British attitudes, see Syed Hussein Alatas, *The Myth of the Lazy Native: A Study of the Image of the Malays, Filipinos and Javanese from the 16th to the 20th Century and its Function in the Ideology of Colonial Capitalism* (London: Frank Cass, 1977).

15. Ada's faith in the future of tobacco as an economically successful crop in North Borneo was to prove unfounded.

16. Durian is the Southeast Asian fruit famous for its forbiddingly spiked skin, repellent odour and ambrosial taste.

17. Amoy was a port in southern China.

18. Johore was the southernmost state on the Malay Peninsula, just north of Borneo.

19. The Astana was a building designated as the palace. Perhaps the most famous Astana in Borneo was the Rajah Brooke's, in Sarawak.

20. Sirih is a trailing tropical plant, the pungent leaves of which are chewed.

21. By the end of 1878 the Spanish had taken Sulu and were claiming, finally without success, the eastern part of Borneo as Sulu territory.

22. Hadji, a title of respect, is given to one who has made the greater pilgrimage to Mecca.

23. A creese, or kris, is a variant of a Malay dagger.

24. A popularized reference to Darwin's theory of natural selection.

25. The P&O was the famous Peninsular and Oriental Steam Navigation Company.

26. A victoria was a low carriage with a convertible top, and a higher seat for the driver or coachman, here called a syce.

27. This is an astonishing remark. Ada had clearly not noticed the situation of most of the Chinese in and around Singapore. Different views are provided by James Frances Warren, *Rickshaw Coolie: A People's History of Singapore (1880–1940)* (Singapore: Oxford University Press, 1986), and Carl A. Trocki, *Opium and Empire: Chinese Society in Colonial Singapore, 1800–1910* (Ithaca, NY: Cornell University Press, 1990).

28. Singapore's shipping success had to do both with its key location and with its being a free port.

29. Johore City, the capital of the state of Johore, was on the mainland of the Malay Peninsula, just north of the island of Singapore.

30. Gutta was the Malay name of the juice of certain trees (percha) found throughout the Malay archipelago. A thin film of gutta as a coating could act as a weatherproof barrier. It would be used to coat the early telegraph wires.

31. Ada's optimism about Labuan's future existed in spite of the facts. By the time of her writing most people had accepted that Labuan would never become successful, or even a financially solvent port. In this remark we can surely hear her husband's enthusiasm.

32. Hugh Low was, along with Frank Swettenham, in the pantheon of famous colonial administrators in Southeast Asia. After his time as governor of Labuan, he went on to a highly successful career as the Resident of Perak, arguably the most important of the states in British Malaya.

33. A godown was the British colonial name for a warehouse or store, often located beside the docks.

34. This was the Public Works Department, central to the infrastructure of a British colonial town.

35. Ada arrived in North Borneo in 1883.

36. Farms were, in fact, the term used in Southeast Asia to mean government licences. This farm system was modelled on Singapore, which made up for its being a free port, with neither duties nor taxes, by selling licences (at very high prices) to private businessmen for the right to sell opium or alcohol or to run gambling dens. Unlike Singapore, Sandakan had duties and taxes as well as 'farms', and still had to struggle financially.

37. In the tropics, the punkah was the ubiquitous overhead fan, typically operated by a servant.

38. Ada does not seem to take sufficiently into account that Chinese from different regions of China spoke very different languages, and their common tongue was often Malay.

39. Ada may well have written some of the manuscript when the couple were in London in 1892.
40. Here begins a section, common in late Victorian travel memoirs, on the flora and fauna of the region.
41. Harriet Beecher Stowe, *Uncle Tom's Cabin, or Life among the Lowly* (Boston: John P. Jewett & Company, 1852).
42. Frank Hatton, *North Borneo: Explorations and Adventures on the Equator* (London: Sampson, Low, Marston, Searle & Rivington, 1886).

WORKS CITED OR ALLUDED TO IN THE ORIGINAL TEXT

Beeckman, Daniel, *A Voyage to and from the Island of Borneo* (London: T. Warner and J. Batley, 1718).

Bock, Carl, *The Headhunters of Borneo: A Narrative of Travel up the Mahakkam and down the Barito; Also Journeyings in Sumatra* (1881; reprinted Singapore: Oxford University Press, 1985).

Hatton, Frank, *North Borneo, Explorations and Adventures on the Equator* (London: Sampson, Low, Marsten, Searle & Rivington, 1886).

Hatton, Joseph, *The New Ceylon: Being a Sketch of British North Borneo, or Sabah* (London: Chapman and Hall, 1881).

Piggafetta, Antonio, *The Last Voyage Around the World of Magellan*, 'Translated from the Accounts of Piggafetta' (London: Hakluyt Society, 1874).

St John, Spencer, *The Life of Sir James Brooke, Rajah of Sarawak, from His Personal Papers and Correspondence* (Edinburgh: W. Blackwood and Sons, 1879).

Stowe, Harriet Beecher, *Uncle Tom's Cabin, or Life among the Lowly* (Boston: John P. Jewett and Company, 1852).

Woolley, G. C., 'Mr. F. X. Witti's Last Journey and Death', *Bulletin of the North Borneo State Museum* (Sandakan, 1938).

WORKS CITED BY THE EDITOR

Alatas, Syed Hussein, *The Myth of the Lazy Native: A Study of the Image of the Malays, Filipinos and Javanese from the 16th to the 20th Century and Its Function in the Ideology of Colonial Capitalism* (London: Frank Cass, 1977).

Black, Ian, *A Gambling Style of Government: The Establishment of the Chartered Company's Rule in Sabah, 1878–1915* (Kuala Lumpur: Oxford University Press, 1983).

Burns, P. L., 'Capitalism and the Malay States', in Hamza Alavi, P. L. Burns, G. R. Knight, P. B. Mayer and Doug McEachern, *Capitalism and Colonial Production* (London: Croom Helm, 1982).

Coates, Austin, 'The Philippines National Hero: Rizal in Sandakan', *Sarawak Museum Journal*, 10 (July–December, 1962).

Conrad, Joseph, *Lord Jim* (1899; reprinted New York: New American Library, 1961).

Crisswell, Colin, *Rajah Charles Brooke: Monarch of All He Surveyed* (Kuala Lumpur: Oxford University Press, 1978).

Donop, L. S. von, 'Diary of Mr. L. S. von Donop's Travels in Sabah in 1882', *Sabah Society Journal*, 3 (March 1968).

Hahn, Emily, *James Brooke of Sarawak: A Biography of James Brooke* (London: Arthur Barker, 1953).

Khoo Kay Kim, *The Western Malay States, 1850–1873* (Kuala Lumpur: Oxford University Press, 1974).

King, Victor T., *The Peoples of Borneo* (Oxford: Blackwell, 1993).

Leong, Cecilia, *Sabah: The First Hundred Years* (Kuala Lumpur: Percetakan Nan Yang Muda Sdn Bhd, 1982).

McDougall, Harriette, *Letters from Sarawak; Addressed to a Child* (Norwich: Thomas Priest, 1854).

Mills, L. A., *British Malaya, 1834–67* (Kuala Lumpur: Oxford University Press, 1966).

Mills, Sara, *Discourses of Difference: An Analysis of Women's Travel Writings and Colonialism* (London: Routledge & Kegan Paul, 1991).

Morgan, Susan, *Place Matters: Gendered Geography in Victorian Women's Travel Books about Southeast Asia* (New Brunswick, NJ: Rutgers University Press, 1996).

Noble, Lela Gardner, *Philippine Policy Toward Sabah: A Claim to Independence* (Tucson: University of Arizona Press, 1977).

Payne, Robert, *The White Rajahs of Sarawak* (1960; reprinted Singapore: Oxford University Press, 1986).

Pringle, Robert, *Rajahs and Rebels: The Ibans of Sarawak under Brooke Rule, 1841–1941* (Ithaca, NY: Cornell University Press, 1970).

Pryer, Ada, *A Decade in Borneo* (Hong Kong: Kelly and Walsh Ltd, 1893; London: Hutchinson, 1894).

Pryer, Ada, *Mrs. Pryer in Sabah*, ed. Nicholas Tarling (Auckland: Centre for Asian Studies, University of Auckland, 1989).

Reece, R. H. W., *The Name of Brooke: The End of White Rajah Rule in Sarawak* (Kuala Lumpur: Oxford University Press, 1982).

Rutter, Owen, *British North Borneo: An Account of Its History, Resources and Native Tribes* (London: Constable, 1922).

Singh, D. S. Ranjit, *Brunei 1839–1983: The Problems of Political Survival* (Singapore: Oxford University Press, 1984).

Sullivan, Anwar and Leong, Cecilia (eds), *Commemorative History of Sabah 1881–1981* (Kuala Lumpur: Sabah State Government Centenary Publications Committee, 1981).

Tarling, Nicholas, *British Policy in the Malay Peninsula and Archipelago, 1824–71* (Kuala Lumpur: Oxford University Press, 1969).

Tarling, Nicholas, *Britain, the Brookes, and Brunei* (Kuala Lumpur: Oxford University Press, 1971).

Tarling, Nicholas, *The Burthen, the Risk, and the Glory: A Biography of Sir James Brooke* (Kuala Lumpur: Oxford University Press, 1982).

Thomas, Nicholas, *Colonialism's Culture: Anthropology, Travel and Government* (Cambridge: Polity Press, 1994).

Tregonning, K. G., 'The Elimination of Slavery in North Borneo', *Journal of the Malayan Branch of the Royal Asiatic Society*, 26 (1953).

Tregonning, K. G., 'William Pryer, the Founder of Sandakan', *Journal of the Malayan Branch of the Royal Asiatic Society*, 27 (1954).

Tregonning, K. G., 'A Sandakan Diary of the 1890s', *Sarawak Museum Journal*, 6 (July 1955).

Tregonning, K. G., *Under Chartered Company Rule (North Borneo 1881–1946)* (Singapore: University of Malaya Press, 1958).

Tregonning, K. G., *North Borneo* (London: HMSO, 1960).

Tregonning, K. G., *A History of Modern Sabah: North Borneo, 1881–1963* (Singapore: University of Malaya Press, 1965).

Trocki, Carl, *Opium and Empire: Chinese Society in Colonial Singapore, 1800–1910* (Ithaca, NY: Cornell University Press, 1990).

Wagner, Ulla, *Colonialism and Iban Warfare* (Stockholm: OBE-Tryck, 1972).

Warren, James F., *The North Borneo Chartered Company's Administration of the Bajau, 1878–1909: The Pacification of a Maritime, Nomadic People* (Athens: Ohio University Center for International Studies, 1971).

Warren, James Francis, *Rickshaw Coolie: A People's History of Singapore, 1880–1940* (Singapore: Oxford University Press, 1986).

Wells, Gordon, *Sabah* (Jesselton: Sabah Times Press, 1963).

Winzeler, Robert L. (ed.), *Indigenous Peoples and the State: Politics, Land and Ethnicity in the Malayan Peninsula and Borneo* (New Haven: Yale University Press, 1997).

Wright, L. R., *The Origins of British Borneo* (Hong Kong: Hong Kong University Press, 1970).

Index

In the index AP stands for Ada Pryer and WP stands for William Pryer. Page numbers in *italics* refer to illustrations.